Proof of God's Word

ROBERT L. PATTERSON

PROOF OF GOD'S WORD

This book is written to provide information and motivation to readers. Its purpose is not to render any type of psychological, legal, or professional advice of any kind. The content is the sole opinion and expression of the author, and not necessarily that of the publisher.

Copyright © 2025 by Robert L. Patterson.

All rights reserved. No part of this book may be reproduced, transmitted, or distributed in any form by any means, including, but not limited to, recording, photocopying, or taking screenshots of parts of the book, without prior written permission from the author or the publisher. Brief quotations for noncommercial purposes, such as book reviews, permitted by Fair Use of the U.S. Copyright Law, are allowed without written permissions, as long as such quotations do not cause damage to the book's commercial value. For permissions, write to the publisher, whose address is stated below.

Printed in the United States of America.

ISBN   978-1-64552-286-7   (Paperback)
ISBN   978-1-64552-287-4   (Digital)

Lettra Press books may be ordered through booksellers or by contacting:

Lettra Press LLC
30 N Gould St. Suite 4753
Sheridan, WY 82801
1 307-200-3414 | info@lettrapress.com
www.lettrapress.com

Contents

Inspiration vii
Introduction ix
Acknowledgments xi

The Bible.. 1
Young People... 8
Renegade Christians..13
Unseen World...16
Cowards..22
Jehovah...26
Behaving In The House Of God 29
Prodigal Christians 32
The Responsibility Of Parents And Grandparents 35
Camouflage Christians 40
Are You On The Lord's Side 43
Who Do You Hate: Or Who Do You Love? 46
Salt Is Good..50
Christian's Responsibility To One Another 53
The Church That Christ Is Coming Back After 56
Bishops, Deacons, Elders 60
Plain Talk..69
The Conception, The Birth, And The Death Of Jesus Christ 73
Why People Should Go To The Churches Of Christ......................76
Who Will Go To Heaven 81
Satan And His Dragons 85

Doing The Will Of God From The Heart 90
Straining At Gnats 95
Medicine And Physicians..99
No Time...106
The World..111
Preaching To Save Souls; Or Preaching For A Living....................118
The Trinity...125
The True Vine: The Husbandman: And The Branches 132
Time And Purpose..138
Gazing Into Heaven 155
Hope..163
A Messenger From God..170
What Kind Of Foundation Is Your Spiritual House Built Upon 176
The Truth...183
A Part Of Paul's Spiritual Journey 189
Living A Guiltless Life 199
Prayer To God..210

PROFILE

Robert L. Patterson

Minister For: The North Little Rock Church Of Christ, 1708 Highway 161, North Little Rock, Arkansas

I Am Just A Nobody, Trying To Tell Everybody, About Somebody, Who Can Save Everybody. Appealing To The Lost Souls, To Come To Christ, Through Preaching The Gospel Of Christ Behind Pulpits, Teaching Personal In Home Bible Classes, And Through My Books, **Title**: **Yoking Up To The Gospel Plow To Learn About Jesus Christ**: And My Book, **Title**: **My Life Struggles**, And Through **YouTube**, And Prayerfully, Through The Publication Of This Book Also.

I Am Truly Thankful To The God Of Heaven, For Those Of You Who Have Helped, And Are Helping Me To Share The Gospel Of Christ, To As Many People In The World As Possible Through Your Prayers And Your Support.

PERSONAL

Father: The Late William Elbert Patterson
Mother: The Late Irene Patterson
There Were 18 Children Born Into This Union

Marital Status

Married To A Beautiful Wife, Thelma A. Patterson And We Have 4 Lovely Sons

Religious Works

I Am A Gospel Preacher/Evangelist And Personal Work Developer. I Am The Author Of The Book Titled, **Yoking Up To The Gospel Plow To Learn About Jesus Christ, And** The Book Title, **My Life Struggles**, And I Also Teach The Gospel Of Christ On **YouTube.**

You Can View Us On YouTube: At The North Little Rock Church Of Christ; You Can Also View Us On YouTube By Scanning Our QR Code On Your Cell Phone.

Inspiration

I Was Inspired To Write This Book Because, I Realized That There Are So Many People Rejecting The Words Of God, And The Words Of Jesus Christ, And Those People Are Traveling The Broad Way That Lead To Destruction, So I Decided To Write This Book Hoping That I Can Help As Many People As Possible To Find The Strait Gate That Lead To Eternal Life!

Jesus said, "13 Enter ye in at the strait gate: for wide is the gate, and broad is the way, that leadeth to destruction, and many there be which go in thereat: 14 Because strait is the gate, and narrow is the way, which leadeth unto life, and few there be that find it" Matt 7:13-14.

Christ said, "48 He that rejecteth me, and receiveth not my words, hath one that judgeth him: the word that I have spoken, the same shall judge him in the last day. 49 For I have not spoken of myself; but the Father which sent me, he gave me a commandment, what I should say, and what I should speak. 50 And I know that his commandment is life everlasting: whatsoever I speak therefore, even as the Father said unto me, so I speak" John 12:48-50.

Rejecting The Words Of God, Is Like Putting A Dollar Bill Into A Money Changing Machine And The Machine Reject The Dollar Bill.

When People Hear The Words Of God And Reject It By Not Obeying It, Then God Reject Those People And They Will Not Enter into Eternal Life.

Christ said, "48 He that rejecteth me, and receiveth not my words, hath one that judgeth him: the word that I have spoken, the same shall judge him in the last day" John 12:48.

Introduction

The Object Of This Book Is To Share With All Mankind The Proof Of God's Word, So That The Readers Can Understand That There Are Many Preachers Who Are Saying Things About The Word Of God That They Cannot Prove By The Bible, The Written Word Of God.

Paul said, "7 Therefore, as ye abound in everything, in faith, and utterance, and knowledge, and in all diligence, and in your love to us, see that ye abound in this grace also. 8 I speak not by commandment, but by occasion of the forwardness of others, and to **Prove** the **Sincerity** of your **Love**. 9 For ye know the grace of our Lord Jesus Christ, that, though he was rich, yet for your sakes he became poor, that ye through his poverty might be rich" 2 Cor 8:7-9.

Paul said, "8 For ye were sometimes darkness, but now are ye light in the Lord: walk as children of light: 9 (For the fruit of the Spirit is in all goodness and righteousness and truth;) 10 **Proving** what is **Acceptable** unto the **Lord**. 11 And have no fellowship with the unfruitful works of darkness, but rather reprove them" Eph 5:8-11.

Acknowledgments

Acknowledgement Is Said To Be A Confession Of Appreciation And Compliment.

Therefore, I Want To Confess My True Appreciation To The God Of Heaven For Giving Me The Knowledge To Read And To Understand Christ And The Apostles' Doctrine, And For The Ability To Relate To His People Through The Means Of Writing.

I Want To Give Thanks To My Lovely Wife, Thelma Patterson, For Her Unwavering Commitment; For Her Wisdom, And For Her Knowledge, Having Her Working With Me Has Been Very Inspirational, She Have Inspired Me Greatly And Has Been A Very Good Colleague. For Her; I Am Most Thankful.

I Want To Give A Special Appreciation To My Daddy, Elbert Patterson For His Instructions, And My Mother, Irene Patterson For Her Encouraging Words Of Wisdom, And To The Both Of Them For Loving And Teaching Me And The Rest Of My Brothers And Sisters Not To Let What Other People Say To Or About Us To Cause Us To Deviate From Doing The Right Things.

My Deep Gratitude And Indebtedness Is To You, The Readers Of This Book: I Truly Hope That It Will Inspire You In A Godly Way; To Use This Book As A Guide To Teach Believers In Christ How To Grow Spiritually, And How To Teach Non-believers To Believe In God, In Jesus Christ And His Church.

The Bible

The Bible Is The Book Where People Can Find Scriptures, That Can Help Them To Gain Knowledge From God's Word, So That They Will Be Able To Do His Will.

The Bible Is The World's Most Read Book, It Is The World's Most Popular Book, It Is The World's Most Influential Book, And Yet It Is The World's Most Misunderstood Book.

The Book That Many People Call The Bible; Was Originally Call The Book.

Isaiah said, "16 Seek ye out of the book of the LORD, and read: no one of these shall fail, none shall want her mate: for my mouth it hath commanded, and his spirit it hath gathered them. 17 And he hath cast the lot for them, and his hand hath divided it unto them by line: they shall possess it for ever, from generation to generation shall they dwell therein" Isaiah 34:16-17.

David said, "7 Then said I, Lo, I come: in the volume of the book it is written of me, 8 I delight to do thy will, O my God: yea, thy law is within my heart. 9 I have preached righteousness in the great congregation: lo, I have not refrained my lips, O LORD, thou knowest. 10 I have not hid thy righteousness within my heart; I have declared thy faithfulness and thy salvation: I have not concealed thy lovingkindness and thy truth from the great congregation" Psalms 40:7-10.

The Hebrew writer said, "7 Then said I, Lo, I come (in the volume of the book it is written of me,) to do thy will, O God. 8 Above when he said, Sacrifice and offering and burnt offerings and offering for sin thou wouldest not, neither hadst pleasure therein; which are offered by the law; 9 Then said he, Lo, I come to do thy will, O God. He taketh away the first, that he may establish the second" Heb 10:7-9.

The Bible Teaches In The Old Testament Scriptures; That The Prophets Was Sent By God.

Isaiah said, "11 So shall my word be that goeth forth out of my mouth: it shall not return unto me void, but it shall accomplish that which I please, and it shall prosper in the thing whereto I sent it. 12 For ye shall go out with joy, and be led forth with peace: the mountains and the hills shall break forth before you into singing, and all the trees of the field shall clap their hands. 13 Instead of the thorn shall come up the fir tree, and instead of the brier shall come up the myrtle tree: and it shall be to the LORD for a name, for an everlasting sign that shall not be cut off". Isaiah 55:11-13

Jeremiah said, "20 The anger of the LORD shall not return, until he have executed, and till he have performed the thoughts of his heart: in the latter days ye shall consider it perfectly. 21 I have not sent these prophets, yet they ran: I have not spoken to them, yet they prophesied. 22 But if they had stood in my counsel, and had caused my people to hear my words, then they should have turned them from their evil way, and from the evil of their doings" Jer 23:20-22.

Jeremiah said, "28 The prophet that hath a dream, let him tell a dream; and he that hath my word, let him speak my word faithfully. What is the chaff to the wheat? saith the LORD. 29 Is not my word like as a fire? saith the LORD; and like a hammer that breaketh the rock in pieces?" Jer 23:28-29.

The Bible Teaches In The Old Testament Scriptures; That God Communicated To The Prophets Verbally.

The Bible said, "9 And it came to pass, as Moses entered into the tabernacle, the cloudy pillar descended, and stood at the door of the tabernacle, and the LORD talked with Moses. 10 And all the people saw the cloudy pillar stand at the tabernacle door: and all the people rose up and worshipped, every man in his tent door. 11 And the LORD spake unto Moses face to face, as a man speaketh unto his friend. And he turned again into the camp: but his servant Joshua, the son of Nun, a young man, departed not out of the tabernacle" Ex 33:9-11.

The Bible said, "4 And the LORD spake suddenly unto Moses, and unto Aaron, and unto Miriam, Come out ye three unto the tabernacle of the congregation. And they three came out. 5 And the LORD came down in the pillar of the cloud, and stood in the door of the tabernacle, and called Aaron and Miriam: and they both came forth. 6 And he said, Hear now my words: If there be a prophet among you, I the LORD will make myself known unto him in a vision, and will speak unto him in a dream. 7 My servant Moses is not so, who is faithful in all mine house. 8 With him will I speak mouth to mouth, even apparently, and not in dark speeches; and the similitude of the LORD shall he behold: wherefore then were ye not afraid to speak against my servant Moses? 9 And the anger of the LORD was kindled against them; and he departed" Num 12:4-9.

The Hebrew writer said, "1 God, who at sundry times and in divers manners spake in time past unto the fathers by the prophets" Heb 1:1.

The Bible Teaches In The New Testament Scriptures; That After Christ Died, The Apostles Taught And Sent Gospel Preachers To Preach The Gospel Of Christ, And They Taught Those Preachers To Teach Other Men To Teach And Preach The Gospel Of Christ.

Paul said, "13 For whosoever shall call upon the name of the Lord shall be saved. 14 How then shall they call on him in whom they have not believed? and how shall they believe in him of whom they have not heard? and how shall they hear without a preacher? 15 And how shall they preach, except they be sent? as it is written, How beautiful are the feet of them that preach the gospel of peace, and bring glad tidings of good things" Romans 10:13-15.

Paul said, "1 Paul, an apostle of Jesus Christ by the commandment of God our Saviour, and Lord Jesus Christ, which is our hope; 2 Unto Timothy, my own son in the faith: Grace, mercy, and peace, from God our Father and Jesus Christ our Lord. 3 As I besought thee to abide still at Ephesus, when I went into Macedonia, that thou mightest charge some that they teach no other doctrine, 4 Neither give heed to fables and endless genealogies, which minister questions, rather than godly edifying which is in faith: so do" 1 Tim 1:1-4.

Paul said, "1 I charge thee therefore before God, and the Lord Jesus Christ, who shall judge the quick and the dead at his appearing and his kingdom; 2 Preach the word; be instant in season, out of season; reprove, rebuke, exhort with all longsuffering and doctrine. 3 For the time will come when they will not endure sound doctrine; but after their own lusts shall they heap to themselves teachers, having itching ears; 4 And they shall turn away their ears from the truth, and shall be turned unto fables" 2 Tim 4:1-4.

Paul said, "4 To Titus, mine own son after the common faith: Grace, mercy, and peace, from God the Father and the Lord Jesus Christ our Saviour. 5 For this cause left I thee in Crete, that thou shouldest set in order the things that are wanting, and ordain elders in every city, as I had appointed thee" Titus 1:4-5.

The Bible Teaches In The New Testament Scriptures; That After The Apostles Died, The Gospel Preachers Taught And Sent Preachers To Preach The Gospel Of Christ.

Paul said, "1 Thou therefore, my son, be strong in the grace that is in Christ Jesus. 2 And the things that thou hast heard of me among many witnesses, the same commit thou to faithful men, who shall be able to teach others also. 3 Thou therefore endure hardness, as a good soldier of Jesus Christ" 2 Tim 2:1-3.

Paul said, "16 All scripture is given by inspiration of God, and is profitable for doctrine, for reproof, for correction, for instruction in righteousness: 17 That the man of God may be perfect, throughly furnished unto all good works" 2 Tim 3:16-17.

The Bible Teaches In The New Testament Scriptures; That The Prophecy Came In Old Time By Holy Men Of God As They Were Moved By The Holy Ghost

Peter said, "20 Knowing this first, that no prophecy of the scripture is of any private interpretation. 21 For the prophecy came not in old time by the will of man: but holy men of God spake as they were moved by the Holy Ghost" 2 Peter 1:20-21.

The Bible Teaches In The New Testament Scriptures; That All Scripture Was Written For Our Learning, And To Bring Us To Christ.

Paul said, "4 For whatsoever things were written aforetime were written for our learning, that we through patience and comfort of the scriptures might have hope. 5 Now the God of patience and consolation grant you to be likeminded one toward another according to Christ Jesus: 6 That ye may with one mind and one mouth glorify God, even the Father of our Lord Jesus Christ" Rom 15:4-6.

Paul said, "22 But the scripture hath concluded all under sin, that the promise by faith of Jesus Christ might be given to them that believe. 23 But before faith came, we were kept under the law, shut up unto the faith which should afterwards be revealed. 24 Wherefore the law was our schoolmaster to bring us unto Christ, that we might be justified by faith. 25 But after that faith is come, we are no longer under a schoolmaster. 26 For ye are all the children of God by faith in Christ Jesus" Gal 3:22-26.

According To The Bible There Are Many False Modern Day Preachers Who Are Lying, When They Tell People That The God Of Heaven Speak To Them Verbally; And These False Preachers

Have Turned People From The Churches Of Christ Through Their Lies; And They Are Causing Many Souls To Go Down The Broad Way That Lead To Destruction.

Isaiah said, "18 For thus saith the LORD that created the heavens; God himself that formed the earth and made it; he hath established it, he created it not in vain, he formed it to be inhabited: I am the LORD; and there is none else. 19 I have not spoken in secret, in a dark place of the earth: I said not unto the seed of Jacob, Seek ye me in vain: I the LORD speak righteousness, I declare things that are right" Isaiah 45:18-19.

Isaiah said, "16 Come ye near unto me, hear ye this; I have not spoken in secret from the beginning; from the time that it was, there am I: and now the Lord GOD, and his Spirit, hath sent me. 17 Thus saith the LORD, thy Redeemer, the Holy One of Israel; I am the LORD thy God which teacheth thee to profit, which leadeth thee by the way that thou shouldest go" Isaiah 48:16-17.

Paul said, "29 For I know this, that after my departing shall grievous wolves enter in among you, not sparing the flock. 30 Also of your own selves shall men arise, speaking perverse things, to draw away disciples after them" Acts 20:29-30.

John said, "18 Little children, it is the last time: and as ye have heard that antichrist shall come, even now are there many antichrists; whereby we know that it is the last time. 19 They went out from us, but they were not of us; for if they had been of us, they would no doubt have continued with us: but they went out, that they might be made manifest that they were not all of us" 1 John 2:18-19.

John said, "1 Beloved, believe not every spirit, but try the spirits whether they are of God: because many false prophets are gone out into the world" 1 John 4:1.

Jude said, "4 For there are certain men crept in unawares, who were before of old ordained to this condemnation, ungodly men, turning the grace of our God into lasciviousness, and denying the only Lord God, and our Lord Jesus Christ" Jude 1:4.

Christ said, "13 Enter ye in at the strait gate: for wide *is* the gate, and broad *is* the way, that leadeth to destruction, and many there be which go in thereat" Matt 7:13.

Young People

Making A Plea To Young People

I Am Written This Epistle Hoping To Inspire All Young People And To Give Them The Courage To Develop Themselves Into Great Men And Women For God, Therefore We As Adults Ought To Take Great Pride In Our Young People, Because They Are Our Future Generations, And We Must Do All In Our Power To Help Them To Maintain Their Integrity.

Young People Do Not Allow Anyone To Tell You That You Cannot Be Perfect As Christians In The Sight Of God.

Christ said, "48 Be ye therefore perfect, even as your Father which is in heaven is perfect" Matt 5:48.

Paul said, "13 Till we all come in the unity of the faith, and of the knowledge of the Son of God, unto a perfect man, unto the measure of the stature of the fulness of Christ: 14 That we henceforth be no more children, tossed to and fro, and carried about with every wind of doctrine, by the sleight of men, and cunning craftiness, whereby they lie in wait to deceive; 15 But speaking the truth in love, may grow up into him in all things, which is the head, even Christ" Eph 4:13-15.

Paul said, "26 Even the mystery which hath been hid from ages and from generations, but now is made manifest to his saints: 27 To whom God would make known what is the riches of the glory of this mystery among the Gentiles; which is Christ in you, the hope of glory: 28 Whom we preach, warning every man, and teaching every man in all wisdom; that we may present every man perfect in Christ Jesus: 29 Whereunto I also labour, striving according to his working, which worketh in me mightily" Col 1:26-29.

Paul said, "12 Epaphras, who is one of you, a servant of Christ, saluteth you, always labouring fervently for you in prayers, that ye may stand perfect and complete in all the will of God" Col 4:12.

Paul said, "15 Let us therefore, as many as be perfect, be thus minded: and if in any thing ye be otherwise minded, God shall reveal even this unto you. 16 Nevertheless, whereto we have already attained, let us walk by the same rule, let us mind the same thing" Phil 3:15-16.

The Hebrew writer said, "20 Now the God of peace, that brought again from the dead our Lord Jesus, that great shepherd of the sheep, through the blood of the everlasting covenant, 21 Make you perfect in every good work to do his will, working in you that which is wellpleasing in his sight, through Jesus Christ; to whom be glory for ever and ever. Amen" Heb 13:20-21.

Young People; Do Not Allow The Biases And Prejudices Of Other To Make You Look Down, And Have Disbelief In Yourselves.

Paul said, "12 Let no man despise thy youth; but be thou an example of the believers, in word, in conversation, in charity, in spirit, in faith, in purity" 1 Tim 4:12.

Paul said, "13 I can do all things through **Christ** which strengtheneth **me**" Phil 4:13.

Young People; Learn To Love God With All Your Heart, And Obey Him While You Are Young.

The Bible said, "5 And thou shalt love the LORD thy God with all thine heart, and with all thy soul, and with all thy might. 6 And these words, which I command thee this day, shall be in thine heart: 7 And thou shalt teach them diligently unto thy children, and shalt talk of them when thou sittest in thine house, and when thou walkest by the way, and when thou liest down, and when thou risest up" Deut 6:5-7.

Solomon said, "5 Trust in the LORD with all thine heart; and lean not unto thine own understanding. 6 In all thy ways acknowledge him, and he shall direct thy paths" Prov 3:5-6.

Solomon said, "1 **Remember** now thy **Creator** in the days of thy **Youth**, while the evil days come **Not**, nor the years draw **nigh**, when thou shalt **say, I** have no pleasure in **Them**" Eccl 12:1.

Young People; Learn To Be Very Courageous In All Your Ways As Children Of The Most High God.

Joshua said, "7 Only be thou strong and very courageous, that thou mayest observe to do according to all the law, which Moses my servant commanded thee: turn not from it to the right hand or to the left, that thou mayest prosper whithersoever thou goest" Josh 1:7.

Young People; David Is A Good Example To Demonstrate Great Courage For Young, And Old People To Follow After.

The Bible said, "32 And David said to Saul, Let no man's heart fail because of him; thy servant will go and fight with this Philistine. 33 And Saul said to David, thou art not able to go against this Philistine to fight with him: for thou art but a Youth, and he a man of war from his Youth" 1 Sam 17:32-33.

The Bible said, "34 And David said unto Saul, Thy servant kept his father's sheep, and there came a Lion, and a Bear, and took a lamb out of the flock: 35 And I went out after him, and smote him, and delivered it out of his Mouth: and when he arose against me, I caught him by his beard, and smote Him, and slew Him. 36 thy servant slew both the Lion and the Bear: and this Uncircumcised Philistine shall be as one of Them, seeing he hath defied the armies of the Living God.

37 David said moreover, The LORD that delivered me out of the Paw of the Lion, and out of the Paw of the Bear, he will deliver me out of the Hand of this Philistine. And Saul said unto David, Go, And The LORD Be With Thee" 1 Sam 17:34-37.

The Bible said, "38 And Saul armed David with his armour, and he put an helmet of brass upon his head; also he armed him with a coat of mail. 39 And David girded his sword upon his armour, and he assayed to go; for he had not proved it. And David said unto Saul, I cannot go with these; for I have not proved them. And David put them off him. 40 And he took his staff in his hand, and chose him five smooth stones out of the brook, and put them in a shepherd's bag which he had, even in a scrip; and his sling was in his hand: and he drew near to the Philistine" 1 Sam 17:38-40.

The Bible said, "41 And the Philistine came on and drew near unto David; and the man that bare the shield went before him. 42 And when the Philistine looked about, and saw David, he disdained him: for he was but a youth, and ruddy, and of a fair countenance" 1 Sam 17:41-42.

The Bible said, "45 Then said David to the Philistine, Thou comest to me with a sword, and with a spear, and with a shield: but I come to thee in the name of the LORD of hosts, the God of the armies of Israel, whom thou hast defied. 46 This day will the LORD deliver thee into mine hand; and I will smite thee, and take thine head from thee; and I will give the carcases of the host of the Philistines this day unto the fowls of the air, and to the wild beasts of the earth; that all the earth may know that there is a God in Israel" 1 Sam 17:45-46.

The Bible said, "49 And David put his hand in his bag, and took thence a stone, and slang it, and smote the Philistine in his forehead, that the stone sunk into his forehead; and he fell upon his face to the earth. 50 So David prevailed over the Philistine with a sling and with a stone, and smote the Philistine, and slew him; but there was no sword in the hand of David. 51 Therefore David ran, and stood upon the Philistine, and took his sword, and drew it out of the sheath thereof, and slew him, and cut off his head therewith. And when the Philistines saw their champion was dead, they fled" 1 Sam 17:49-51.

Young People; Keep God Commandments: Honor Your Father And Mother; And You Will Live Long On The Earth.

Solomon said, "1 My son, forget not my law; but let thine heart keep my commandments: 2 For length of days, and long life, and peace, shall they add to thee. 3 Let not mercy and truth forsake thee: bind them about thy neck; write them upon the table of thine heart" Prov 3:1-3.

Paul said, "1 Children, obey your parents in the Lord: for this is right. 2 Honour thy father and mother; (which is the first commandment with promise;) 3 That it may be well with thee, and thou mayest live long on the earth" Eph 6:1-3.

The Bible said, "11 When I was a child, I spake as a child, I understood as a child, I thought as a child: but when I became a man, I put away childish things" 1 Cor 13:11.

David said, "25 I have been young, and now am old; yet have I not seen the Righteous Forsaken, nor his seed Begging Bread. 26 He is ever merciful, and lendeth; and his seed is blessed. 27 Depart from Evil, and do good; and dwell for Evermore. 28 For the LORD loveth judgment, And Forsaketh Not His Saints; they are preserved for ever: but the seed of the wicked shall be Cut Off" Psalms 37:25-28.

Renegade Christians

Renegade Christians; Are Rebels Who Have Rejected Doing Things As God Require.

Renegade Christians; Have Rejected And Turn From The Words Of God, And God Considered Them As DOGS And HOGS That Has Turn Back To Their Old Ways.

Solomon said, "10 The great God that formed all things both rewardeth the fool, and rewardeth transgressors. 11 As a dog returneth to his vomit, so a fool returneth to his folly. 12 Seest thou a man wise in his own conceit (pride)? there is more hope of a fool than of him" Prov 26:10-12.

Paul said, "8 Howbeit then, when ye knew not God, ye did service unto them which by nature are no gods. 9 But now, after that ye have known God, or rather are known of God, how turn ye again to the weak and beggarly elements, whereunto ye desire again to be in bondage?" Gal 4:8-9.

Peter said, "21 For it had been better for them not to have known the way of righteousness, than, after they have known it, to turn from the holy commandment delivered unto them. 22 But it is happened unto them according to the true proverb, The dog is turned to his own vomit again; and the sow that was washed to her wallowing in the mire" 2 Peter 2:21-22.

Renegade Christians; Reject To Give, As God Require.

Malachi said, "7 Even from the days of your fathers ye are gone away from mine ordinances, and have not kept them. Return unto me, and I will return unto you, saith the LORD of hosts. But ye said, Wherein shall we return? 9 Ye are cursed with a curse: for ye have robbed me, even this whole nation. 10 Bring ye all the tithes into the storehouse, that there may be meat in mine house, and prove me now herewith, saith the LORD of hosts, if I will not open you the windows of heaven, and pour you out a blessing, that there shall not be room enough to receive it" Mal 3:7, 9-10.

The Bible said, "1 But a certain man named Ananias, with Sapphira his wife, sold a possession, 2 And kept back part of the price, his wife also being privy to it, and brought a certain part, and laid it at the apostles' feet. 5 And Ananias hearing these words fell down, and gave up the ghost: and great fear came on all them that heard these things. 9 Then Peter said unto her, How is it that ye have agreed together to tempt the Spirit of the Lord? behold, the feet of them which have buried thy husband are at the door, and shall carry thee out. 10 Then fell she down straightway at his feet, and yielded up the ghost: and the young men came in, and found her dead, and, carrying her forth, buried her by her husband" Acts 5:1-2,5,9-10.

Renegade Christians; Reject The Truth, Of The Gospel Of Christ.

Paul said, "1 O foolish Galatians, who hath bewitched you, that ye should not obey the truth, before whose eyes Jesus Christ hath been evidently set forth, crucified among you? 2 This only would I learn of you, Received ye the Spirit by the works of the law, or by the hearing of faith? 3 Are ye so foolish? having begun in the Spirit, are ye now made perfect by the flesh? 4 Have ye suffered so many things in vain? if it be yet in vain" Gal 3:1-4.

Renegade Christians; Reject God's Requirements, Concerning Murmur, And Murmurings.

The Bible said, "10 And the LORD said unto Moses, Bring Aaron's rod again before the testimony, to be kept for a token against the rebels; and thou shalt quite take away their murmurings from me, that they die not" Num 17:10.

The Bible said, "43 Jesus therefore answered and said unto them, Murmur not among yourselves" John 6:43.

Paul said, "10 Neither murmur ye, as some of them also murmured, and were destroyed of the destroyer" 1 Cor 10:10.

God said, "36 Like as I pleaded with your fathers in the wilderness of the land of Egypt, so will I plead with you, saith the Lord GOD" Ezek 20:36.

Renegade Gospel Preachers; Have Rejected, And Perverted The Gospel Of Christ.

Paul said, "6 I marvel that ye are so soon removed from him that called you into the grace of Christ unto another gospel: 7 Which is not another; but there be some that trouble you, and would pervert the gospel of Christ. 8 But though we, or an angel from heaven, preach any other gospel unto you than that which we have preached unto you, let him be accursed. 9 As we said before, so say I now again, If any man preach any other gospel unto you than that ye have received, let him be accursed. 10 For do I now persuade men, or God? or do I seek to please men? for if I yet pleased men, I should not be the servant of Christ" Gal 1:6-10.

Unseen World

Faithful Christians Are **Living In The Spiritual Unseen World**

Faithful Christians Has Been Transforms From Their Old Fleshly Way Of Life, Into A New Spiritual Unseen Way Of Life.

Faithful Christians In The Unseen World Are Lively Stones.

Peter said, "5 Ye also, as lively stones, are built up a spiritual house, an holy priesthood, to offer up spiritual sacrifices, acceptable to God by Jesus Christ" 1 Peter 2:5.

Faithful Christians Must Know That The Same Things That They Did To Become Christians Are The Same Things That They Must Do To Inherit Eternal Life.

To Become A Faithful Christian, A Person Must Be Taught The Word Of God.

Jesus said, "44 No Man Can Come To Me, Except The Father Which Hath Sent Me Draw Him: And I Will Raise Him Up At The Last Day. It Is Written In The Prophets, 45 And They Shall Be All Taught Of God. Every Man Therefore That Hath Heard, And Hath Learned Of The Father, Cometh Unto Me" John 6:44-45.

To Become A Faithful Christian, A Person Must Hear The Word Of God.

The Bible said, "27 And it came to pass, as he spake these things, a certain woman of the company lifted up her voice, and said unto him, Blessed is the womb that bare thee, and the paps which thou hast sucked. 28 But he said, Yea rather, blessed are they that hear the word of God, and keep it" Luke 11:27-28.

To Become A Faithful Christian, A Person Must Believe Jesus Christ Is The Son Of God.

Jesus said, "37 If I do not the works of my Father, believe me not. 38 But if I do, though ye believe not me, believe the works: that ye may know, and believe, that the Father is in me, and I in him" John 10:37-38.

The Bible said, "36 And as they went on their way, they came unto a certain water: and the eunuch said, See, here is water; what doth hinder me to be baptized? 37 And Philip said, If thou believest with all thine heart, thou mayest. And he answered and said, I believe that Jesus Christ is the Son of God" Acts 8:36-37.

To Become A Faithful Christian, A Person Must Repent Of Their Sins.

The Bible said, "1 There were present at that season some that told him of the Galilaeans, whose blood Pilate had mingled with their sacrifices. 2 And Jesus answering said unto them, Suppose ye that these Galilaeans were sinners above all the Galilaeans, because they suffered such things? 3 I tell you, Nay: but, except ye repent, ye shall all likewise perish" Luke 13:1-3.

The Bible said, "37 Now When They Heard This, They Were Pricked In Their Heart, And Said Unto Peter And To The Rest Of The Apostles, Men And Brethren, What Shall We Do? 38 Then Peter Said Unto Them, Repent, And Be Baptized Every One Of You In The Name Of Jesus Christ For The Remission Of Sins, And Ye Shall Receive The Gift Of The Holy Ghost" Acts 2:37-38.

To Become A Faithful Christian, A Person Must Confess, That They Believe That Jesus Christ Is The Son Of God.

Jesus said, "32 Whosoever Therefore Shall Confess Me Before Men, Him Will I Confess Also Before My Father Which Is In Heaven. 33 But Whosoever Shall Deny Me Before Men, Him Will I Also Deny Before My Father Which Is In Heaven" Matthew 10:32-33.

The Bible said, "36 And as they went on their way, they came unto a certain water: and the eunuch said, See, here is water; what doth hinder me to be baptized? 37 And Philip said, If thou believest with all thine heart, thou mayest. And he answered and said, I believe that Jesus Christ is the Son of God" Acts 8:36-37.

Paul said, "9 That if thou shalt confess with thy mouth the Lord Jesus, and shalt believe in thine heart that God hath raised him from the dead, thou shalt be saved. 10 For with the heart man believeth unto righteousness; and with the mouth confession is made unto salvation. 11 For the scripture saith, Whosoever believeth on him shall not be ashamed" Romans 10:9-11.

To Become A Faithful Christian, A Person Must Be Baptized For The Remission Of Their Sins.

The Bible said, "18 And Jesus came and spake unto them, saying, All power is given unto me in heaven and in earth. 19 Go ye therefore, and teach all nations, baptizing them in the name of the Father, and of the Son, and of the Holy Ghost: 20 Teaching them to observe all things whatsoever I have commanded you: and, lo, I am with you alway, even unto the end of the world. Amen" Matt 28:18-20.

Jesus said, "15 And he said unto them, Go ye into all the world, and preach the gospel to every creature. 16 He that believeth and is baptized shall be saved; but he that believeth not shall be damned" Mark 16:15-16.

Faithful Unseen Christians Have Learned How To Suffer As Christians.

Peter said, "15 But let none of you suffer as a murderer, or as a thief, or as an evildoer, or as a busybody in other men's matters. 16 Yet if any man suffer as a Christian, let him not be ashamed; but let him glorify God on this behalf" 1 Peter 4:15-16.

In Order For Faithful Christians, To Gain Eternal Life They Must Remain Faithful Unto Death!

John said, "13 And I heard a voice from heaven saying unto me, Write, Blessed are the dead which die in the Lord from henceforth: Yea, saith the Spirit, that they may rest from their labours; and their works do follow them" Rev 14:13.

The Bible said, "21 Then said Jesus again unto them, I go my way, and ye shall seek me, and shall die in your sins: whither I go, ye cannot come. 23 And he said unto them, Ye are from beneath; I am from above: ye are of this world; I am not of this world. 24 I said therefore unto you, that ye shall die in your sins: for if ye believe not that I am he, ye shall die in your sins" John 8:21, 23-24.

In Order For Faithful Christians, To Gain Eternal Life They Must Get Rid Of Everything That Cause Them To Sin!

The Hebrew writer said, "1 Wherefore seeing we also are compassed about with so great a cloud of witnesses, let us lay aside every weight, and the sin which doth so easily beset us, and let us run with patience the race that is set before us, 2 Looking unto Jesus the author and finisher of our faith; who for the joy that was set before him endured the cross, despising the shame, and is set down at the right hand of the throne of God. 3 For consider him that endured such contradiction of sinners against himself, lest ye be wearied and faint in your minds" Heb 12:1-3.

Paul said, "1 Let a man so account of us, as of the ministers of Christ, and stewards of the mysteries of God. 2 Moreover it is required in stewards, that a man be found faithful" 1 Cor 4:1-2.

Furthermore Paul said, "57 But thanks be to God, which giveth us the victory through our Lord Jesus Christ. 58 Therefore, my beloved brethren, be ye stedfast, unmoveable, always abounding in the work of the Lord, forasmuch as ye know that your labour is not in vain in the Lord" 1 Cor 15:57-58.

In Order For Faithful Christians To Gain Eternal Life, They Must Not Forsake The Assemblies Of God!

The Bible said, "23 And they shall teach my people the difference between the holy and profane, and cause them to discern between the unclean and the clean. 24 And in controversy they shall stand in judgment; and they shall judge it according to my judgments: and they shall keep my laws and my statutes in all mine assemblies; and they shall hallow my sabbaths. 25 And they shall come at no dead person to defile themselves: but for father, or for mother, or for son, or for daughter, for brother, or for sister that hath had no husband, they may defile themselves" Ezek 44:23-25.

Josh said, "15 And if it seem evil unto you to serve the LORD, choose you this day whom ye will serve; whether the gods which your fathers served that were on the other side of the flood, or the gods of the Amorites, in whose land ye dwell: but as for me and my house, we will serve the LORD. 16 And the people answered and said, God forbid that we should forsake the LORD, to serve other gods; 17 For the LORD our God, he it is that brought us up and our fathers out of the land of Egypt, from the house of bondage, and which did those great signs in our **sight**, and preserved us in all the way wherein we went, and among all the people through whom we passed" Josh 24:15-17:

The Hebrew writer said, "25 Not forsaking the assembling of ourselves together, as the manner of some is; but exhorting one another: and so much the more, as ye see the day approaching. 26 For if we sin wilfully after that we have received the knowledge of the truth, there remaineth no more sacrifice for sins, 27 But a certain fearful looking for of judgment and fiery indignation, which shall devour the adversaries" Heb 10:25-27.

Faithful Christians Who Live And Die In The Spiritual Unseen World, Will Gain Eternal Life!

Jesus said, "28 Come unto me, all ye that labour and are heavy laden, and I will give you rest. 29 Take my yoke upon you, and learn of me; for I am meek and lowly in heart: and ye shall find rest unto your souls.

30 For my yoke is easy, and my burden is light" Matt 11:28-30.

John said, "13 And I heard a voice from heaven saying unto me, Write, Blessed *are* the dead which die in the Lord from henceforth: Yea, saith the Spirit, that they may rest from their labours; and their works do follow them" Rev 14:13.

Cowards

Cowards Are People Who Lacks Courage In Facing Truth, Danger, Difficulty, Or Pain, And They Are Easily Frightened.

Reuben Could Have Saved Joseph From Been Sold To Those Midianites Merchantmen, If He Had Of Had The Courage To Stand Up Against His Brothers.

The Bible said, "21 And Reuben heard it, and he delivered him out of their hands; and said, Let us not kill him. 22 And Reuben said unto them, Shed no blood, but cast him into this pit that is in the wilderness, and lay no hand upon him; that he might rid him out of their hands, to deliver him to his father again. 23 And it came to pass, when Joseph was come unto his brethren, that they stript Joseph out of his coat, his coat of many colours that was on him; 24 And they took him, and cast him into a pit: and the pit was empty, there was no water in it. 28 Then there passed by Midianites merchantmen; and they drew and lifted up Joseph out of the pit, and sold Joseph to the Ishmeelites for twenty pieces of silver: and they brought Joseph into Egypt" Gen 37:21-24, 28.

When Moses Gave Joshua The Charge To Lead The People Of Israel To Jordan, He Told Him To Be Strong And Of Good Courage, And Fear Not.

The Bible said, "1 And Moses went and spake these words unto all Israel. 3 The LORD thy God, he will go over before thee, and he will destroy these nations from before thee, and thou shalt possess them:

and Joshua, he shall go over before thee, as the LORD hath said. 6 Be strong and of a good courage, fear not, nor be afraid of them: for the LORD thy God, he it is that doth go with thee; he will not fail thee, nor forsake thee. 7 And Moses called unto Joshua, and said unto him in the sight of all Israel, Be strong and of a good courage: for thou must go with this people unto the land which the LORD hath sworn unto their fathers to give them; and thou shalt cause them to inherit it. 8 And the LORD, he it is that doth go before thee; he will be with thee, he will not fail thee, neither forsake thee: fear not, neither be dismayed" Deut 31:1,3,6-8.

Saul Lost His Kingship, Because He Did Not Have The Courage To Obey God; Instead He Feared The People, And Obeyed Their Voice.

The Bible said, "19 Wherefore then didst thou not obey the voice of the LORD, but didst fly upon the spoil, and didst evil in the sight of the LORD? 23 For rebellion is as the sin of witchcraft, and stubbornness is as iniquity and idolatry. Because thou hast rejected the word of the LORD, he hath also rejected thee from being king. 24 And Saul said unto Samuel, I have sinned: for I have transgressed the commandment of the LORD, and thy words: because I feared the people, and obeyed their voice" 1 Sam 15:19, 23-24.

David Prove His Courage To Saul, By Killing Goliath, The Philistine.

The Bible said, "22 And David left his carriage in the hand of the keeper of the carriage, and ran into the army, and came and saluted his brethren. 23 And as he talked with them, behold, there came up the champion, the Philistine of Gath, Goliath by name, out of the armies of the Philistines, and spake according to the same words: and David heard them. 24 And all the men of Israel, when they saw the man, fled from him, and were sore afraid. 32 And David said to Saul, Let no man's heart fail because of him; thy servant will go and fight with this Philistine" 1 Sam 17:22-24, 32.

Cowardly Preacher Are Afraid To Tell People The Truth, That There Is Only One Church, And That That One Church, Is The Church Of Christ.

Christ said, "18 And I say also unto thee, That thou art Peter, and upon this rock I will build my church; and the gates of hell shall not prevail against it" Matt 16:18.

Paul said, "4 There is one body, and one Spirit, even as ye are called in one hope of your calling; 5 One Lord, one faith, one baptism" Eph 4:4-5.

Paul said, "18 And he is the head of the body, the church: who is the beginning, the firstborn from the dead; that in all things he might have the preeminence. 24 Who now rejoice in my sufferings for you, and fill up that which is behind of the afflictions of Christ in my flesh for his body's sake, which is the church" Col 1:18, 24:

Paul said, "16 Salute one another with an holy kiss. The churches of Christ salute you" Romans 16:16.

There Are Many Cowardly Christians, Who Will Not Allow Themselves To Believe In Jesus.

Christ said, "1 Let not your heart be troubled: ye believe in God, believe also in me. 2 In my Father's house are many mansions: if it were not so, I would have told you. I go to prepare a place for you. 3 And if I go and prepare a place for you, I will come again, and receive you unto myself; that where I am, there ye may be also" John 14:1-3.

Christ said, "38 He that believeth on me, as the scripture hath said, out of his belly shall flow rivers of living water" John 7:38.

Christ said, "37 If I do not the works of my Father, believe me not. 38 But if I do, though ye believe not me, believe the works: that ye may know, and believe, that the Father is in me, and I in him" John 10:37-38.

Satan Caused Many Gospel Preachers To Close The Doors To Their Congregations, Because They Did Not Have The Courage To Stand Against Him In The Evil Days Of Covic-19

Christ said, "13 But woe unto you, scribes and Pharisees, hypocrites! for ye shut up the kingdom of heaven against men: for ye neither go in *yourselves*, neither suffer ye them that are entering to go in" Matt 23:13.

Jehovah

The Bible Teaches That People Should Hear And Keep The Words Of God.

Hearing And Keeping The Word Of God; Mean To Hear And Do Whatever He Say.

The Bible said, "27 And it came to pass, as he spake these things, a certain woman of the company lifted up her voice, and said unto him, Blessed is the womb that bare thee, and the paps which thou hast sucked. 28 But he said, Yea rather, blessed are they that hear the word of God, and keep it" Luke 11:27-28.

Paul Beg The Brethren In The Church In Corinth, To Speak The Same Thing Concerning The Word Of God.

Paul said, "10 Now I beseech you, brethren, by the name of our Lord Jesus Christ, that ye all speak the same thing, and *that* there be no divisions among you; but *that* ye be perfectly joined together in the same mind and in the same judgment" 1 Cor 1:10.

God Told Moses, That He Was Known To Abraham, Isaac, And Jacob, By The Name Of God Almighty.

The Bible said, "2 And God spake unto Moses, and said unto him, I am the LORD: 3 And I appeared unto Abraham, unto Isaac, and unto

Jacob, by *the name of* God Almighty, but by my name JEHOVAH was I not known to them" Exodus 6:2-3.

God Told Moses, That His Name Is To Be Called God Unto All Generations.

The Bible said, "15 And God said moreover unto Moses, Thus shalt thou say unto the children of Israel, The LORD God of your fathers, the God of Abraham, the God of Isaac, and the God of Jacob, hath sent me unto you: this is my name for ever, and this is my memorial unto all generations" Exodus 3:15.

David Prayed To God, Against Those That Was Against Them.

David said, "15 So persecute them with thy tempest, and make them afraid with thy storm. 16 Fill their faces with shame; that they may seek thy name, O LORD. 17 Let them be confounded and troubled for ever; yea, let them be put to shame, and perish: 18 That men may know that thou, whose name alone is JEHOVAH, art the most high over all the earth" Psalms 83:15-18.

Isaiah Prayed To God Giving Him Thanks For Salvation And He Called Him God In Two Difference Languages, He Called Him God And He Called Him JEHOVAH.

The Bible said, "2 Behold, **God** *is* my salvation; I will trust, and not be afraid: for the LORD

JEHOVAH is my strength and my song; he also is become my salvation" Isaiah 12:2.

When Abraham Was Going To Sacrifice His Son, He Told Him That God Will Provide Himself A Lamb. Now Let Us Keep In Mind That God Was Not Known To Abraham, By The Name JEHOVAH.

The Bible said, "7 And Isaac spake unto Abraham his father, and said, My father: and he said, Here am I, my son. And he said, Behold the fire and the wood: but where is the lamb for a burnt offering? 8 And Abraham said, My son, God will provide himself a lamb for a burnt offering: so they went both of them together" Gen 22:7-8.

When Jesus Was Crucified, He Cried Out To God, Saying In Our Language, My God, My God.

The Bible said, "46 And about the ninth hour Jesus cried with a loud voice, saying, Eli, Eli, lama sabachthani? that is to say, My God, my God, why hast thou forsaken me?" Matt 27:46.

I Stand In The Defense Of The Word Of God, As Did The Prophet's, And I Stand In The Defense Of Christ, The Same As Did The Apostles Of Christ!

Peter said, "11 If any man speak, let him speak as the oracles of God; if any man minister, let him do it as of the ability which God giveth: that God in all things may be glorified through Jesus Christ, to whom be praise and dominion for ever and ever. Amen" 1 Peter 4:11.

Paul said, "7 Even as it is meet for me to think this of you all, because I have you in my heart; inasmuch as both in my bonds, and in the defence and confirmation of the gospel, ye all are partakers of my grace. 8 For God is my record, how greatly I long after you all in the bowels of Jesus Christ. 16 The one preach Christ of contention, not sincerely, supposing to add affliction to my bonds: 17 But the other of love, knowing that I am set for the defence of the gospel" Phil 1:7-8, 16-17.

Behaving In The House Of God

Men And Women Must Behaved Themselves In The House Of God, According To The Scripture.

Peter said, "11 If any man speak, let him speak as the oracles of God; if any man minister, let him do it as of the ability which God giveth: that God in all things may be glorified through Jesus Christ, to whom be praise and dominion for ever and ever. Amen" 1 Peter 4:11.

Paul said, "16 All scripture is given by inspiration of God, and is profitable for doctrine, for reproof, for correction, for instruction in righteousness: 17 That the man of God may be perfect, throughly furnished unto all good works" 2 Tim 3:16-17.

The Bible Teaches, That It Is Absolutely A Sin For Women To Ask A Preacher Questions During Worship Services, Without The Permission Of The Preacher.

The Bible said, "12 And it came to pass, as she continued praying before the LORD, that Eli marked her mouth. 13 Now Hannah, she spake in her heart; only her lips moved, but her voice was not heard: therefore Eli thought she had been drunken. 14 And Eli said unto her, How long wilt thou be drunken? put away thy wine from thee. 15 And Hannah answered and said, No, my lord, I am a woman of a sorrowful spirit: I have drunk neither wine nor strong drink, but have poured out my soul before the LORD" 1 Sam 1:12-15.

Paul said, "34 Let your women keep silence in the churches: for it is not permitted unto them to speak; but they are commanded to be under obedience, as also saith the law. 35 And if they will learn any thing, let them ask their husbands at home: for it is a shame for women to speak in the church" 1 Cor 14:34-35.

Some May Ask, What About Women Singing And Praying In The Congregations Of The Churches Of Christ? The Answer Is Singing And Praying Is Not Questioning And Teaching.

David said, "1 Make a joyful noise unto God, <u>all ye lands</u>: 2 Sing forth the honour of his name: make his praise glorious: Psalms 66:1-2.

Paul said, "19 Speaking to yourselves in psalms and hymns and spiritual songs, singing and making melody in your heart to the Lord; 20 Giving thanks always for all things unto God and the Father in the name of our Lord Jesus Christ; 21 Submitting yourselves one to another in the fear of God" Eph 5:19-21.

The Bible Teaches That If A Husband And His Wife Want To Correct A Preacher During Worship, They Must Wait Until The Worship Service Is Over.

The Bible Teaches That When Aquila And Priscilla Wanted To Correct Apollos, They Waited Until The Worship Service Was Over, And Then They Talked With Him Privately.

The Bible said, "24 And a certain Jew named Apollos, born at Alexandria, an eloquent (effortless) man, and mighty in the scriptures, came to Ephesus. 25 This man was instructed in the way of the Lord; and being fervent (enthusiastic) in the spirit, he spake and taught diligently the things of the Lord, knowing only the baptism of John. 26 And he began to speak boldly in the synagogue: whom when Aquila and Priscilla had heard, they took him unto *them*, and expounded unto him the way of God more perfectly" Acts 18:24-26.

The Bible Teaches, That God Wants Us To Keep Confusion Out Of The Congregations Of The Churches Of Christ, And The Way To Do That Is To Keep Our Conversations In Order As We Are Authorize By The Bible.

Paul said, "26 How is it then, brethren? when ye come together, every one of you hath a psalm, hath a doctrine, hath a tongue, hath a revelation, hath an interpretation. Let all things be done unto edifying. 27 If any man speak in an unknown tongue, let it be by two, or at the most by three, and that by course; and let one interpret. 28 But if there be no interpreter, let him keep silence in the church; and let him speak to himself, and to God. 29 Let the prophets speak two or three, and let the other judge. 30 If any thing be revealed to another that sitteth by, let the first hold his peace. 31 For ye may all prophesy one by one, that all may learn, and all may be comforted" 1 Cor 14:26-31.

Furthermore Paul said, "33 For God is not the author of confusion, but of peace, as in all churches of the saints. 40 Let all things be done decently and in order" 1 Cor 14:33, 40.

Jesus said, "26 But the Comforter, which is the Holy Ghost, whom the Father will send in my name, he shall teach you all things, and bring all things to your remembrance, whatsoever I have said unto you. 27 Peace I leave with you, my peace I give unto you: not as the world giveth, give I unto you. Let not your heart be troubled, neither let it be afraid" John 14:26-27.

Jesus said, "50 Salt is good: but if the salt have lost his saltness, wherewith will ye season it? Have salt in yourselves, and have peace one with another" Mark 9:50.

Peter said, "11 Let him eschew evil, and do good; let him seek peace, and ensue it. 12 For the eyes of the Lord are over the righteous, and his ears are open unto their prayers: but the face of the Lord is against them that do evil" 1 Peter 3:11-12.

Prodigal Christians

Prodigal Christians; Are Christians Who Have Left The Congregations Of The Churches Of Christ, And They Are Wasting Their Lives And Their Souls By Living In Sin.

The Prodigal Son Left His Father's House, And Immediately He Went Away And Wasted Everything That He Had.

The Bible said, "11 And he said, A certain man had two sons: 12 And the younger of them said to his father, Father, give me the portion of goods that falleth to me. And he divided unto them his living. 13 And not many days after the younger son gathered all together, and took his journey into a far country, and there wasted his substance with riotous living" Luke 15:11-13.

The Bible said, "14 And when he had spent all, there arose a mighty famine in that land; and he began to be in want. 15 And he went and joined himself to a citizen of that country; and he sent him into his fields to feed swine. 16 And he would fain have filled his belly with the husks that the swine did eat: and no man gave unto him" Luke 15:14-16.

Some Christians Were Not Fortunate Or Lucky Enough, To Come To Themselves And Go Back To God, Before It Was Too Late.

The Bible said, "17 And when he came to himself, he said, How many hired servants of my father's have bread enough and to spare, and I perish with hunger! 18 I will arise and go to my father, and will say unto him, Father, I have sinned against heaven, and before thee, 19 And am no more worthy to be called thy son: make me as one of thy hired servants" Luke 15:17-19.

Prodigal Christians; Should Repent And Return To The Congregation, Confess Their Sins, And The Congregation Should Rejoice, And Be Happy With Them.

The Bible said, "20 And he arose, and came to his father. But when he was yet a great way off, his father saw him, and had compassion, and ran, and fell on his neck, and kissed him.21 And the son said unto him, Father, I have sinned against heaven, and in thy sight, and am no more worthy to be called thy son. 22 But the father said to his servants, Bring forth the best robe, and put it on him; and put a ring on his hand, and shoes on his feet: 23 And bring hither the fatted calf, and kill it; and let us eat, and be merry: 24 For this my son was dead, and is alive again; he was lost, and is found. And they began to be merry" Luke 15:20-24.

Unlike The Prodigal Son Brother, All Christians Should Receive The Prodigal Christians Back To The House Of God, With Pure Joy.

The Bible said, "25 Now his elder son was in the field: and as he came and drew nigh to the house, he heard musick and dancing. 26 And he called one of the servants, and asked what these things meant. 27 And he said unto him, Thy brother is come; and thy father hath killed the fatted calf, because he hath received him safe and sound. 28 And he was angry, and would not go in: therefore came his father out, and intreated him. 29 And he answering said to his father, Lo, these many years do I serve thee, neither transgressed I at any time thy commandment: and yet thou never gavest me a kid, that I might make merry with my friends: 30 But as soon as this thy son was come, which hath devoured thy living with harlots, thou hast killed for him the fatted calf. 31 And he said unto him, Son, thou art ever with me, and all that I have is thine. 32 It was meet that we should make merry, and be glad: for this thy brother was dead, and is alive again; and was lost, and is found" Luke 15:25-32.

Prodigal Christians; Who Have Repented And Have Return To The Congregations, It Is Possible For Them To Remain Faithful To God For The Rest Of Their Lives.

Paul said, "10 I beseech thee for my son Onesimus, whom I have begotten in my bonds: 11 Which in time past was to thee unprofitable, but now profitable to thee and to me: 12 Whom I have sent again: thou therefore receive him, that is, mine own bowels: 13 Whom I would have retained with me, that in thy stead he might have ministered unto me in the bonds of the gospel: 14 But without thy mind would I do nothing; that thy benefit should not be as it were of necessity, but willingly. 15 For perhaps he therefore departed for a season, that thou shouldest receive him for ever; 16 Not now as a servant, but above a servant, a brother beloved, specially to me, but how much more unto thee, both in the flesh, and in the Lord? 17 If thou count me therefore a partner, receive him as myself. 18 If he hath wronged thee, or oweth thee ought, put that on mine account" Philem 1:10-18.

There Are Some Prodigal Christians; Who Have Crucified To Themselves The Son Of God, And It Is Impossible To Renew Those Christians Again Unto Repentance.

The Hebrew writer said, "4 For it is impossible for those who were once enlightened, and have tasted of the heavenly gift, and were made partakers of the Holy Ghost, 5 And have tasted the good word of God, and the powers of the world to come, 6 If they shall fall away, to renew them again unto repentance; seeing they crucify to themselves the Son of God afresh, and put him to an open shame" Heb 6:4-6.

Just As The Prodigal Son Father Met Him When He Returned Home, That Is The Same Way That God Will Do To All Prodigal Christians, Who Will Return To Him.

James said, "7 Submit yourselves therefore to God. Resist the devil, and he will flee from you.

8 Draw nigh to God, and he will draw nigh to you. Cleanse your hands, ye sinners; and purify your hearts, ye double minded" James 4:7-8.

The Responsibility Of Parents And Grandparents

Parents And Grandparents Are Responsible For Teaching Their Children To Love God.

The Bible said, "1 Now these are the commandments, the statutes, and the judgments, which the LORD your God commanded to teach you, that ye might do them in the land whither ye go to possess it: 5 And thou shalt love the LORD thy God with all thine heart, and with all thy soul, and with all thy might. 6 And these words, which I command thee this day, shall be in thine heart: 7 And thou shalt teach them diligently unto thy children, and shalt talk of them when thou sittest in thine house, and when thou walkest by the way, and when thou liest down, and when thou risest up" Deut 6:1, 5-7.

The Bible said, "1 Remember now thy Creator in the days of thy youth, while the evil days come not, nor the years draw nigh, when thou shalt say, I have no pleasure in them; 2 While the sun, or the light, or the moon, or the stars, be not darkened, nor the clouds return after the rain" Eccl 12:1-2.

Parents And Grandparents Are Responsible For Teaching Their Children The Holy Scriptures.

Paul said, "5 When I call to remembrance the unfeigned faith that is in thee, which dwelt first in thy grandmother Lois, and thy mother Eunice; and I am persuaded that in thee also" 2 Tim 1:5.

Paul said, "14 But continue thou in the things which thou hast learned and hast been assured of, knowing of whom thou hast learned them; 15 And that from a child thou hast known the holy scriptures, which are able to make thee wise unto salvation through faith which is in Christ Jesus" 2 Tim 3:14-15.

Parents And Grandparents Are Responsible For Teaching Their Children The Way That They Should Go In Life.

Solomon said, "6 Train up a child in the way he should go" Prov 22:6.

Solomon said, "10 My son, if sinners entice thee, consent thou not. 11 If they say, Come with us, let us lay wait for blood, let us lurk privily for the innocent without cause: 12 Let us swallow them up alive as the grave; and whole, as those that go down into the pit: 13 We shall find all precious substance, we shall fill our houses with spoil: 14 Cast in thy lot among us; let us all have one purse: 15 My son, walk not thou in the way with them; refrain thy foot from their path: 16 For their feet run to evil, and make haste to shed blood" Prov 1:10-16.

Paul said, "4 And, ye fathers, provoke not your children to wrath: but bring them up in the nurture and admonition of the Lord" Eph 6:4.

Parents And Grandparents Are Responsible For Teaching Their Children That Children Are To Be Born In A Home With A Father That Is A Man, And A Mother That Is A Woman, That Is Married To Each Other.

The Bible said, "1 And Adam knew Eve his wife; and she conceived, and bare Cain, and said, I have gotten a man from the LORD. 2 And she again bare his brother Abel. And Abel was a keeper of sheep, but Cain was a tiller of the ground" Gen 4:1-2.

The Bible said, "21 And Isaac intreated the LORD for his wife, because she was barren: and the LORD was intreated of him, and Rebekah his wife conceived. 22 And the children struggled together within her; and she said, If it be so, why am I thus? And she went to enquire of the LORD. 23 And the LORD said unto her, Two nations are in thy womb, and two manner of people shall be separated from thy bowels; and the one people shall be stronger than the other people; and the elder shall serve the younger. 24 And when her days to be delivered were fulfilled, behold, there were twins in her womb. 25 And the first came out red, all over like an hairy garment; and they called his name Esau. 26 And after that came his brother out, and his hand took hold on Esau's heel; and his name was called Jacob: and Isaac was threescore years old when she bare them" Gen 25:21-26.

The Bible said, "19 And they rose up in the morning early, and worshipped before the LORD, and returned, and came to their house to Ramah: and Elkanah knew Hannah his wife; and the LORD remembered her. 20 Wherefore it came to pass, when the time was come about after Hannah had conceived, that she bare a son, and called his name Samuel, saying, Because I have asked him of the LORD" 1 Sam 1:19-20.

Parents And Grandparents Are Responsible For Teaching Their Children, That They Must Not Get Involved With Any Type Of Unmarried Sexual Activities.

Paul said, "1 Now concerning the things whereof ye wrote unto me: It is good for a man not to touch a woman. 2 Nevertheless, to avoid fornication, let every man have his own wife, and let every woman have her own husband"1 Cor 7:1-2.

Paul said, "13 Meats for the belly, and the belly for meats: but God shall destroy both it and them. Now the body is not for fornication, but for the Lord; and the Lord for the body. 18 Flee fornication. Every sin that a man doeth is without the body; but he that committeth fornication sinneth against his own body. 19 What? know ye not that your body is the temple of the Holy Ghost which is in you, which ye have of God, and ye are not your own? 20 For ye are bought with a price: therefore glorify God in your body, and in your spirit, which are God's" 1 Cor 6:13, 18-20.

Parents And Grandparents Are Responsible To Teach And To Discipline Their Children In An Effort, To Save Their Souls From Going To Hell.

Solomon said, "18 Chasten thy son while there is hope, and let not thy soul spare for his crying. 19 A man of great wrath shall suffer punishment: for if thou deliver him, yet thou must do it again. 20 Hear counsel, and receive instruction, that thou mayest be wise in thy latter end. 21 There are many devices in a man's heart; nevertheless the counsel of the LORD, that shall stand" Prov 19:18-21.

Solomon said, "13 Withhold not correction from the child: for if thou beatest him with the rod, he shall not die. 14 Thou shalt beat him with the rod, and shalt deliver his soul from hell. 15 My son, if thine heart be wise, my heart shall rejoice, even mine" Prov 23:13-15.

Solomon said, "15 The rod and reproof give wisdom: but a child left to himself bringeth his mother to shame. 16 When the wicked are multiplied, transgression increaseth: but the righteous shall see their fall. 17 Correct thy son, and he shall give thee rest; yea, he shall give delight unto thy soul" Prov 29:15-17.

Parents And Grandparents Are Responsible For Being Examples For Their Children, And They Are To Teach Them To Be Examples To Others.

Solomon said, "8 My son, hear the instruction of thy father, and forsake not the law of thy mother: 9 For they shall be an ornament of grace unto thy head, and chains about thy neck" Prov 1:8-9.

Solomon said, "1 My son, if thou wilt receive my words, and hide my commandments with thee; 2 So that thou incline thine ear unto wisdom, and apply thine heart to understanding; 3 Yea, if thou criest after knowledge, and liftest up thy voice for understanding; 4 If thou seekest her as silver, and searchest for her as for hid treasures; 5 Then shalt thou understand the fear of the LORD, and find the knowledge of God" Prov 2:1-5.

Solomon said, "1 My son, forget not my law; but let thine heart keep my commandments: 2 For length of days, and long life, and peace, shall they add to thee. 3 Let not mercy and truth forsake thee: bind them about thy neck; write them upon the table of thine heart: 4 So shalt thou find favour and good understanding in the sight of God and man. 5 Trust in the LORD with all thine heart; and lean not unto thine own understanding. 6 In all thy ways acknowledge him, and he shall direct thy paths" Prov 3:1-6.

Solomon said, "11 My son, despise not the chastening of the LORD; neither be weary of his correction: 12 For whom the LORD loveth he correcteth; even as a father the son in whom he delighteth. 13 Happy is the man that findeth wisdom, and the man that getteth understanding. 14 For the merchandise of it is better than the merchandise of silver, and the gain thereof than fine gold" Prov 3:11-14.

Paul said, "12 Let no man despise thy youth; but be thou an example of the believers, in word, in conversation, in charity, in spirit, in faith, in purity. 13 Till I come, give attendance to reading, to exhortation, to doctrine" 1 Tim 4:12-13.

Paul said, "3 The aged women likewise, that they be in behaviour as becometh holiness, not false accusers, not given to much wine, teachers of good things; 4 That they may teach the young women to be sober, to love their husbands, to love their children, 5 To be discreet, chaste, keepers at home, good, obedient to their own husbands, that the word of God be not blasphemed" Titus 2:3-5.

Camouflage Christians

Camouflage: Is To Disguise One's Self: So That They Can Blend In With The Crowd Without Being Detected Or Notice.

One Of The Reasons That The Spiritual Warfare Is So Difficult To Fight, Is Because The Enemies Have Camouflaged Themselves In Among The Christians.

Paul said, "12 But what I do, that I will do, that I may cut off occasion (The Boasting) from them which desire occasion (The Boasting); that wherein they glory, they may be found even as we. 13 For such are false apostles, deceitful workers, transforming themselves into the apostles of Christ. 14 And no marvel; for Satan himself is transformed into an angel of light. 15 Therefore it is no great thing if his ministers also be transformed as the ministers of righteousness; whose end shall be according to their works" 2 Cor 11:12-15.

Jude said, "3 Beloved, when I gave all diligence to write unto you of the common salvation, it was needful for me to write unto you, and exhort you that ye should earnestly contend for the faith which was once delivered unto the saints. 4 For there are certain men crept in unawares, who were before of old ordained to this condemnation, ungodly men, turning the grace of our God into lasciviousness, and denying the only Lord God, and our Lord Jesus Christ. 5 I will therefore put you in remembrance, though ye once knew this, how that the Lord, having saved the people out of the land of Egypt, afterward destroyed them that believed not" Jude 1:3-5.

Some Unfaithful Christians Have Left Their Congregations, And Have Camouflage Themselves In With A Different Congregation; So That If They Do Not Attend Worship, Or If They Neglect To Give As They Should, They Believe That They Will Not Be Detected Or Notice.

The Bible said, "41 And Jesus sat over against the treasury, and beheld how the people cast money into the treasury: and many that were rich cast in much. 42 And there came a certain poor widow, and she threw in two mites, which make a farthing. 43 And he called unto him his disciples, and saith unto them, Verily I say unto you, That this poor widow hath cast more in, than all they which have cast into the treasury: 44 For all they did cast in of their abundance; but she of her want did cast in all that she had, even all her living" Mark 12:41-44.

Some Christians Have Camouflage Themselves In With The Unbelievers, Trying To Blend In With Them, Hoping That They Will Not Be Detected Or Notice.

Jesus said, "14 ye are the light of the world. a city that is set on an hill cannot be hid. 15 neither do men light a candle, and put it under a bushel, but on a candlestick; and it giveth light unto all that are in the house. 16 let your light so shine before men, that they may see your good works, and glorify your father which is in heaven" Matt 5:14-16.

Paul said, "14 Be ye not unequally yoked together with unbelievers: for what fellowship hath righteousness with unrighteousness? and what communion hath light with darkness? 17 Wherefore come out from among them, and be ye separate, saith the Lord, and touch not the unclean thing; and I will receive you, 18 And will be a Father unto you, and ye shall be my sons and daughters, saith the Lord Almighty" 2 Cor 6:14, 17-18.

The Apostle Peter Tried To Camouflage Himself In With The Unbelievers, When Christ Was Been Lead To The Judgment Hall.

The Bible said, "69 Now Peter sat without in the palace: and a damsel came unto him, saying, Thou also wast with Jesus of Galilee. 70 But he denied before them all, saying, I know not what thou sayest. 71 And when he was gone out into the porch, another maid saw him, and said unto them that were there, This fellow was also with Jesus of Nazareth. 72 And again he denied with an oath, I do not know the man. 73 And after a while came unto him they that stood by, and said to Peter, Surely thou also art one of them; for thy speech bewrayeth thee. 74 Then began he to curse and to swear, saying, I know not the man. And immediately the cock crew" Matt 26:69-74.

The Bible said, "11 but when Peter was come to Antioch, I withstood him to the face, because he was to be blamed. 12 for before that certain came from James, he did eat with the gentiles: but when they were come, he withdrew and separated himself, fearing them which were of the circumcision" Gal 2:11-12.

Camouflage Christians; Should Repent For Disguising Themselves; And Turn Back To God.

The Bible said, "18 Come now, and let us reason together, saith the LORD: though your sins be as scarlet, they shall be as white as snow; though they be red like crimson, they shall be as wool.

The Bible said, "19 If ye be willing and obedient, ye shall eat the good of the land:

20 But if ye refuse and rebel, ye shall be devoured with the sword: for the mouth of the LORD hath spoken it" Isaiah 1:18-20.

David said, "4 The ungodly are not so: but are like the chaff which the wind driveth away. 5 Therefore the ungodly shall not stand in the judgment, nor sinners in the congregation of the righteous. 6 For the LORD knoweth the way of the righteous: but the way of the ungodly shall perish" Psalms 1:4-6.

Are You On The Lord's Side

The True Meaning Of Being On Someone's Side, Means, That You Are In Agreement With Someone.

The Bible said, "3 Can two walk together, except they be agreed?" Amos 3:3.

The Bible said, "26 Then Moses stood in the gate of the camp, and said, Who is on the LORD'S side? let him come unto me. And all the sons of Levi gathered themselves together unto him.

27 And he said unto them, Thus saith the LORD God of Israel, Put every man his sword by his side, and go in and out from gate to gate throughout the camp, and slay every man his brother, and every man his companion, and every man his neighbour. 28 And the children of Levi did according to the word of Moses: and there fell of the people that day about three thousand men" Ex 32:26-28.

Elijah said, "37 Hear me, O LORD, hear me, that this people may know that thou art the LORD God, and that thou hast turned their heart back again. 38 Then the fire of the LORD fell, and consumed the burnt sacrifice, and the wood, and the stones, and the dust, and licked up the water that was in the trench. 39 And when all the people saw it, they fell on their faces: and they said, The LORD, he is the God; the LORD, he is the God. 40 And Elijah said unto them, Take the prophets of Baal; let not one of them escape. And they took them: and

Elijah brought them down to the brook Kishon, and slew them there" 1 Kings 18:37-40.

The People That Do Not Know God, And Do Not Love Him, Worship Him Ignorantly.

Paul said, "23 For as I passed by, and beheld your devotions, I found an altar with this inscription, TO THE UNKNOWN GOD. Whom therefore ye ignorantly worship, him declare I unto you. 24 God that made the world and all things therein, seeing that he is Lord of heaven and earth, dwelleth not in temples made with hands; 25 Neither is worshipped with men's hands, as though he needed any thing, seeing he giveth to all life, and breath, and all things; 26 And hath made of one blood all nations of men for to dwell on all the face of the earth, and hath determined the times before appointed, and the bounds of their habitation; 27 That they should seek the Lord, if haply they might feel after him, and find him, though he be not far from every one of us: 28 For in him we live, and move, and have our being; as certain also of your own poets have said, For we are also his offspring" Acts 17:23-28.

The People That Love God, They Do Things To Prove That They Love Him.

The Bible said, "15 So when they had dined, Jesus saith to Simon Peter, Simon, son of Jonas, lovest thou me more than these? He saith unto him, Yea, Lord; thou knowest that I love thee. He saith unto him, Feed my lambs. 16 He saith to him again the second time, Simon, son of Jonas, lovest thou me? He saith unto him, Yea, Lord; thou knowest that I love thee. He saith unto him, Feed my sheep. 17 He saith unto him the third time, Simon, son of Jonas, lovest thou me? Peter was grieved because he said unto him the third time, Lovest thou me? And he said unto him, Lord, thou knowest all things; thou knowest that I love thee. Jesus saith unto him, Feed my sheep" John 21:15-17.

People That Love God, Show Themselves Approved Unto Him.

Paul said, "10 Proving what is acceptable unto the Lord" Eph 5:10.

Paul said, "1 I beseech you therefore, brethren, by the mercies of God, that ye present your bodies a living sacrifice, holy, acceptable unto God, which is your reasonable service. 2 And be not conformed to this world: but be ye transformed by the renewing of your mind, that ye may prove what is that good, and acceptable, and perfect, will of God" Romans 12:1-2.

Paul said, "15 Study to shew thyself approved unto God, a workman that needeth not to be ashamed, rightly dividing the word of truth. 16 But shun profane and vain babblings: for they will increase unto more ungodliness. 17 And their word will eat as doth a canker: of whom is Hymenaeus and Philetus; 18 Who concerning the truth have erred, saying that the resurrection is past already; and overthrow the faith of some" 2 Tim 2:15-18.

Christ said, "7 Ye hypocrites, well did Esaias prophesy of you, saying, 8 This people draweth nigh unto me with their mouth, and honoureth me with their lips; but their heart is far from me. 9 But in vain they do worship me, teaching for doctrines the commandments of men" Matt 15:7-9.

Who Do You Hate: Or Who Do You Love?

The People That Love God, Will Worship And Serve Him, As He Commanded Them.

Jesus said, "24 No man can serve two masters: for either he will hate the one, and love the other; or else he will hold to the one, and despise the other. Ye cannot serve God and mammon" Matt 6:24.

Joshua said, "15 And if it seem evil unto you to serve the LORD, choose you this day whom ye will serve; whether the gods which your fathers served that were on the other side of the flood, or the gods of the Amorites, in whose land ye dwell: but as for me and my house, we will serve the LORD. 16 And the people answered and said, God forbid that we should forsake the LORD, to serve other gods" Josh 24:15-16.

The Bible said, "21 And Elijah came unto all the people, and said, How long halt ye between two opinions? if the LORD be God, follow him: but if Baal, then follow him. And the people answered him not a word" 1 Kings 18:21.

People Can Tell Which God They Hate Or Love, By Doing The Things That They Say.

Jesus said, "15 If ye love me, keep my commandments. 23 Jesus answered and said unto him, If a man love me, he will keep my words: and my

Father will love him, and we will come unto him, and make our abode with him. 24 He that loveth me not keepeth not my sayings: and the word which ye hear is not mine, but the Father's which sent me" John 14:15, 23-24.

Paul said, "16 Know ye not, that to whom ye yield yourselves servants to obey, his servants ye are to whom ye obey; whether of sin unto death, or of obedience unto righteousness? 17 But God be thanked, that ye were the servants of sin, but ye have obeyed from the heart that form of doctrine which was delivered you. 18 Being then made free from sin, ye became the servants of righteousness" Romans 6:16-18.

Loving People Do Loving Thing, From The Goodness That Is In Their Heats; Evil People Do Evil Things, From The Hatred That Is In Their Hearts.

Christ said, "35 A good man out of the good treasure of the heart bringeth forth good things: and an evil man out of the evil treasure bringeth forth evil things. 36 But I say unto you, That every idle word that men shall speak, they shall give account thereof in the day of judgment. 37 For by thy words thou shalt be justified, and by thy words thou shalt be condemned" Matt 12:35-37.

Luke said, "34 For Where Your Treasure Is, There Will Your Heart Be Also. 35 Let Your Loins Be Girded About, And Your Lights Burning" Luke 12:34-35.

Elijah said, "37 Hear me, O LORD, hear me, that this people may know that thou art the LORD God, and that thou hast turned their heart back again. 38 Then the fire of the LORD fell, and consumed the burnt sacrifice, and the wood, and the stones, and the dust, and licked up the water that was in the trench. 39 And when all the people saw it, they fell on their faces: and they said, The LORD, he is the God; the LORD, he is the God. 40 And Elijah said unto them, Take the prophets of Baal; let not one of them escape. And they took them: and Elijah brought them down to the brook Kishon, and slew them there" 1 Kings 18:37-40.

The People That Do Not Know God, And Do Not Love Him, Worship Him Ignorantly.

Paul said, "23 For as I passed by, and beheld your devotions, I found an altar with this inscription, TO THE UNKNOWN GOD. Whom therefore ye ignorantly worship, him declare I unto you. 24 God that made the world and all things therein, seeing that he is Lord of heaven and earth, dwelleth not in temples made with hands; 25 Neither is worshipped with men's hands, as though he needed any thing, seeing he giveth to all life, and breath, and all things; 26 And hath made of one blood all nations of men for to dwell on all the face of the earth, and hath determined the times before appointed, and the bounds of their habitation; 27 That they should seek the Lord, if haply they might feel after him, and find him, though he be not far from every one of us: 28 For in him we live, and move, and have our being; as certain also of your own poets have said, For we are also his offspring" Acts 17:23-28.

The People That Love God, They Do Things, To Prove That They Love Him.

The Bible said, "15 So when they had dined, Jesus saith to Simon Peter, Simon, son of Jonas, lovest thou me more than these? He saith unto him, Yea, Lord; thou knowest that I love thee. He saith unto him, Feed my lambs. 16 He saith to him again the second time, Simon, son of Jonas, lovest thou me? He saith unto him, Yea, Lord; thou knowest that I love thee. He saith unto him, Feed my sheep. 17 He saith unto him the third time, Simon, son of Jonas, lovest thou me? Peter was grieved because he said unto him the third time, Lovest thou me? And he said unto him, Lord, thou knowest all things; thou knowest that I love thee. Jesus saith unto him, Feed my sheep" John 21:15-17.

The People That Love God Show Themselves Approved Unto Him.

Paul said, "10 Proving what is acceptable unto the Lord" Eph 5:10.

Paul said, "1 I beseech you therefore, brethren, by the mercies of God, that ye present your bodies a living sacrifice, holy, acceptable unto God, which is your reasonable service. 2 And be not conformed to this world: but be ye transformed by the renewing of your mind, that ye may prove what is that good, and acceptable, and perfect, will of God" Romans 12:1-2.

Paul said, "15 Study to shew thyself approved unto God, a workman that needeth not to be ashamed, rightly dividing the word of truth. 16 But shun profane and vain babblings: for they will increase unto more ungodliness. 17 And their word will eat as doth a canker: of whom is Hymenaeus and Philetus; 18 Who concerning the truth have erred, saying that the resurrection is past already; and overthrow the faith of some" 2 Tim 2:15-18.

Salt Is Good

Salt Is A Mineral Composed Primarily Of Sodium Chloride, Which Can Be Used To Preserve Food.

In The Old Days Sharecroppers Used Salt To Preserve Their Meat, In What They Called Smoke Houses.

In The Spiritual Sense Christians Have A Twofold Responsibility: They Are The Salt Of The Earth That Can Save People Souls From Going To Hell; They Also Have The Light Of Life, That Can Lead People Souls To Heaven.

Christians Have The Ingredients Within Themselves, That Can Save The Entire World.

Christ said, "13 Ye are the **salt** of the earth: but if the salt have lost his savour, wherewith shall it be salted? it is thenceforth good for nothing, but to be cast out, and to be trodden under foot of men.14 Ye are the light of the world. A city that is set on an hill cannot be hid. 15 Neither do men light a candle, and put it under a bushel, but on a candlestick; and it giveth light unto all that are in the house. 16 Let your light so shine before men, that they may see your good works, and glorify your Father which is in heaven" Matt 5:13-16.

Christians Must Make Sure That They Do Not Lose Their Salt.

The Bible said, "49 For every one shall be salted with fire, and every sacrifice shall be salted with salt. 50 Salt is good: but if the salt have lost his saltness, wherewith will ye season it? Have salt in yourselves, and have peace one with another" Mark 9:49-50.

The Bible said, "34 Salt is good: but if the salt have lost his savour, wherewith shall it be seasoned? 35 It is neither fit for the land, nor yet for the dunghill; but men cast it out. He that hath ears to hear, let him hear" Luke 14:34-35.

Paul said, "5 Walk in wisdom toward them that are without, redeeming the time. 6 Let your speech be alway with grace, seasoned with salt, that ye may know how ye ought to answer every man" Col 4:5-6.

Christians Must Realized That They Cannot Survive As Faithful Christians, While Living Two Difference Lives.

James said, "12 Can the fig tree, my brethren, bear olive berries? either a vine, figs? so can no fountain both yield salt water and fresh" James 3:12.

James said, "7 Submit yourselves therefore to God. Resist the devil, and he will flee from you.

8 Draw nigh to God, and he will draw nigh to you. Cleanse your hands, ye sinners; and purify your hearts, ye double minded" James 4:7-8.

Christians Must Maintain Their Salt, So That They Can Help To Restore Other Christians Who Have Falling, To Regain Steadfast In The Faith.

Solomon said, "9 Two are better than one; because they have a good reward for their labour. 10 For if they fall, the one will lift up his fellow: but woe to him that is alone when he falleth; for he hath not another to help him up. 11 Again, if two lie together, then they have heat: but how can one be warm alone? 12 And if one prevail against him, two shall withstand him; and a threefold cord is not quickly broken" Eccl 4:9-12.

The Bible said, "31 And The Lord Said, Simon, Simon, Behold, Satan Hath Desired To Have You, That He May Sift You As Wheat: 32 But I Have Prayed For Thee, That Thy Faith Fail Not: And When Thou Art <u>Converted</u>, Strengthen Thy Brethren" Luke 22:31-32.

Christians Must Always Remember, That It Does Not Matter How Much We Help Others, It Is God That Get The Victory.

Paul said, "6 I have planted, Apollos watered; but God gave the increase. 7 So then neither is he that planteth any thing, neither he that watereth; but God that giveth the increase. 8 Now he that planteth and he that watereth are one: and every man shall receive his own reward according to his own labour" 1 Cor 3:6-8.

Paul said, "13 I can do all things through Christ which strengtheneth me" Phil 4:13.

Paul said, "57 But thanks be to God, which giveth us the victory through our Lord Jesus Christ. 58 Therefore, my beloved brethren, be ye stedfast, unmoveable, always abounding in the work of the Lord, forasmuch as ye know that your labour is not in vain in the Lord" 1 Cor 15:57-58.

Christian's Responsibility To One Another

There Are Some Gospel Preachers Who Are Avoiding Their Responsibility To Other Gospel Preachers Who They Know Or Believe That They Are In Sin, And They Avoid Fellowshipping With Them Without Trying To Help Those Gospel Preachers To Repent And Turn Back To God. Brethren According To The Scripture Those Gospel Preachers Who Refuse To Help Other Gospel Preachers To Repent Are In Sin Themselves.

The Bible said, "20 Again, When a righteous man doth turn from his righteousness, and commit iniquity, and I lay a stumblingblock before him, he shall die: because thou hast not given him warning, he shall die in his sin, and his righteousness which he hath done shall not be remembered; but his blood will I require at thine hand. 21 Nevertheless if thou warn the righteous man, that the righteous sin not, and he doth not sin, he shall surely live, because he is warned; also thou hast delivered thy soul" Ezek 3:20-21.

Paul said, "1 Brethren, if a man be overtaken in a fault, ye which are spiritual, restore such an one in the spirit of meekness; considering thyself, lest thou also be tempted. 2 Bear ye one another's burdens, and so fulfil the law of Christ. 3 For if a man think himself to be something, when he is nothing, he deceiveth himself. 4 But let every man prove his own work, and then shall he have rejoicing in himself alone, and not in another" Gal 6:1-4.

Paul said, "14 And many of the brethren in the Lord, waxing confident by my bonds, are much more bold to speak the word without fear. 15 Some indeed preach Christ even of envy and strife; and some also of good will: 16 The one preach Christ of contention, not sincerely, supposing to add affliction to my bonds: 17 But the other of love, knowing that I am set for the defence of the gospel. 18 What then? notwithstanding, every way, whether in pretence, or in truth, Christ is preached; and I therein do rejoice, yea, and will rejoice" Phil 1:14-18.

Paul said, "11 And have no fellowship with the unfruitful works of darkness, but rather reprove them" Eph 5:11.

All Gospel Preachers, And All Faithful Christian's Have The Responsibility To Help Their Fellow Christians, When We See Them Struggling With The Burdens Of This Life.

Christ said. "4 For they bind heavy burdens and grievous to be borne, and lay them on men's shoulders; but they themselves will not move them with one of their fingers. 5 But all their works they do for to be seen of men: they make broad their phylacteries, and enlarge the borders of their garments, 6 And love the uppermost rooms at feasts, and the chief seats in the synagogues, 7 And greetings in the markets, and to be called of men, Rabbi, Rabbi" Matt 23:4-7.

Jude said, "21 Keep yourselves in the love of God, looking for the mercy of our Lord Jesus Christ unto eternal life. 22 And of some have compassion, making a difference: 23 And others save with fear, pulling them out of the fire; hating even the garment spotted by the flesh. 24 Now unto him that is able to keep you from falling, and to present you faultless before the presence of his glory with exceeding joy, 25 To the only wise God our Saviour, be glory and majesty, dominion and power, both now and ever. Amen" Jude 1:21-25.

John said, "16 Hereby perceive we the love of God, because he laid down his life for us: and we ought to lay down our lives for the brethren. 17 But whoso hath this world's good, and seeth his brother have need, and shutteth up his bowels of compassion from him, how dwelleth the love of God in him? 18 My little children, let us not love in word, neither in tongue; but in deed and in truth. 19 And hereby we know that we are of the truth, and shall assure our hearts before him" 1 John 3:16-19.

The Hebrew writer said, "1 Wherefore seeing we also are compassed about with so great a cloud of witnesses, let us lay aside every weight, and the sin which doth so easily beset us, and let us run with patience the race that is set before us, 2 Looking unto Jesus the author and finisher of our faith; who for the joy that was set before him endured the cross, despising the shame, and is set down at the right hand of the throne of God. 3 For consider him that endured such contradiction of sinners against himself, lest ye be wearied and faint in your minds" Heb 12:1-3.

The Bible Teaches, That Christ Is Our Example, And We As Christians Are To Follow His Way.

Peter said, "21 For even hereunto were ye called: because Christ also suffered for us, leaving us an example, that ye should follow his steps: 22 Who did no sin, neither was guile found in his mouth: 23 Who, when he was reviled, reviled not again; when he suffered, he threatened not; but committed himself to him that judgeth righteously: 24 Who his own self bare our sins in his own body on the tree, that we, being dead to sins, should live unto righteousness: by whose stripes ye were healed. 25 For ye were as sheep going astray; but are now returned unto the Shepherd and Bishop of your souls" 1 Peter 2:21-25.

Christ said. "3 Take heed to yourselves: If thy brother trespass against thee, rebuke him; and if he repent, forgive him. 4 And if he trespass against thee seven times in a day, and seven times in a day turn again to thee, saying, I repent; thou shalt forgive him" Luke 17:3-4.

Christ said. "19 As many as I love, I rebuke and chasten: be zealous therefore, and repent. 20 Behold, I stand at the door, and knock: if any man hear my voice, and open the door, I will come in to him, and will sup with him, and he with me" Rev 3:19-20.

The Church That Christ Is Coming Back After

Christ Is Coming Back After The Church That He Build.

Christ said, "18 And I say also unto thee, That thou art Peter, and upon this rock I will build my church; and the gates of hell shall not prevail against it. 19 And I will give unto thee the keys of the kingdom of heaven: and whatsoever thou shalt bind on earth shall be bound in heaven: and whatsoever thou shalt loose on earth shall be loosed in heaven" Matt 16:18-19.

David said, "1 Except the LORD build the house, they labour in vain that build it: except the LORD keep the city, the watchman waketh *but* in vain" Psalms 127:1.

Peter said, "5 Ye also, as lively stones, are built up a spiritual house, an holy priesthood, to offer up spiritual sacrifices, acceptable to God by Jesus Christ" 1 Peter 2:5.

Christ Is Coming Back After The Church That He Is The Head Of.

Paul said, "12 For as the body is one, and hath many members, and all the members of that one body, being many, are one body: so also is Christ. 13 For by one Spirit are we all baptized into one body, whether we be Jews or Gentiles, whether we be bond or free; and have been all made to drink into one Spirit. 14 For the body is not one member, but many" 1 Cor 12:12-14.

Paul said, "18 And he is the head of the body, the church: who is the beginning, the firstborn from the dead; that in all things he might have the preeminence. 24 Who now rejoice in my sufferings for you, and fill up that which is behind of the afflictions of Christ in my flesh for his body's sake, which is the church" Col 1:18, 24.

Christ Is Coming Back After His Church, And It Have Salvation In It.

Paul said, "10 Be it known unto you all, and to all the people of Israel, that by the name of Jesus Christ of Nazareth, whom ye crucified, whom God raised from the dead, even by him doth this man stand here before you whole. 11 This is the stone which was set at nought of you builders, which is become the head of the corner. 12 Neither is there salvation in any other: for there is none other name under heaven given among men, whereby we must be saved" Acts 4:10-12.

Paul said, "10 Therefore I endure all things for the elect's sakes, that they may also obtain the salvation which is in Christ Jesus with eternal glory" 2 Tim 2:10.

Christ Is Coming Back After The Church That Wear His Name.

Paul said, "21 Far above all principality, and power, and might, and dominion, and every name that is named, not only in this world, but also in that which is to come: 22 And hath put all things under his feet, and gave him to be the head over all things to the church, 23 Which is his body, the fulness of him that filleth all in all. 25 Husbands, love your wives, even as Christ also loved the church, and gave himself for it" Eph 1:21-23, 25.

Paul said, "28 So ought men to love their wives as their own bodies. He that loveth his wife loveth himself. 29 For no man ever yet hated his own flesh; but nourisheth and cherisheth it, even as the Lord the church: 30 For we are members of his body, of his flesh, and of his bones. 31 For this cause shall a man leave his father and mother, and shall be joined unto his wife, and they two shall be one flesh. 32 This is a great mystery: but I speak concerning Christ and the church. 33 Nevertheless let every one of you in particular so love his wife even as himself; and the wife see that she reverence her husband" Eph 5:28-33.

Christ Is Coming Back After The Kingdom That God Set Up.

Daniel said, "44 And in the days of these kings shall the God of heaven set up a kingdom, which shall never be destroyed: and the kingdom shall not be left to other people, but it shall break in pieces and consume all these kingdoms, and it shall stand for ever" Dan 2:44.

Christ said, "33 But seek ye first the kingdom of God, and his righteousness; and all these things shall be added unto you" Matt 6:33.

Christ Is Coming Back After Those Who Believe; And Work Righteousness Until Death.

The Bible said, "34 Then Peter opened his mouth, and said, Of a truth I perceive that God is no respecter of persons: 35 But in every nation he that feareth him, and worketh righteousness, is accepted with him" Acts 10:34-35.

John said, "13 And I heard a voice from heaven saying unto me, Write, Blessed *are* the dead which die in the Lord from henceforth: Yea, saith the Spirit, that they may rest from their labours; and their works do follow them" Rev 14:13.

Paul said, "24 Then *cometh* the end, when he shall have delivered up the kingdom to God, even the Father; when he shall have put down all rule and all authority and power" 1 Cor 15:24.

Peter said, "10 But the day of the Lord will come as a thief in the night; in the which the heavens shall pass away with a great noise, and the elements shall melt with fervent heat, the earth also and the works that are therein shall be burned up. 11 Seeing then that all these things shall be dissolved, what manner of persons ought ye to be in all holy conversation and godliness" 2 Peter 3:10-11.

Christ Is Coming Back After His Church Without Spot, Wrinkle, Blemish, Or Any Other Sin.

Paul said, "26 That he might sanctify and cleanse it with the washing of water by the word,

27 That he might present it to himself a glorious church, not having spot, or wrinkle, or any such thing; but that it should be holy and without blemish" Eph 5:26-27.

Paul said, "22 But now being made free from sin, and become servants to God, ye have your fruit unto holiness, and the end everlasting life. 23 For the wages of sin is death; but the gift of God is eternal life through Jesus Christ our Lord" Romans 6:22-23.

Paul said, "14 For if we believe that Jesus died and rose again, even so them also which sleep in Jesus will God bring with him. 15 For this we say unto you by the word of the Lord, that we which are alive and remain unto the coming of the Lord shall not prevent them which are asleep. 16 For the Lord himself shall descend from heaven with a shout, with the voice of the archangel, and with the trump of God: and the dead in Christ shall rise first: 17 Then we which are alive and remain shall be caught up together with them in the clouds, to meet the Lord in the air: and so shall we ever be with the Lord. 18 Wherefore comfort one another with these words" 1 Thess 4:14-18.

Bishops, Deacons, Elders

Men And Brethrens, I Would Like To Point Out The Misguided, And False Teaching Concerning The Qualifications Of Bishops; Deacons, And Elders In The Church, Also I Want To Point Out The Dismantling Or The Ceasing Of The Position Of The Elders Of The Church; Since The Perfect Law Of Liberty Have Come, According To The Scripture.

Those Elders Of The Church That Paul Sent For From Ephesus; Were From Different Congregations In Ephesus; Not Just One Congregation, As Some Would Have You To Believe; And Paul Ordained Those Elders To Preach The Word Of God.

The Bible said, "17 And from Miletus he sent to Ephesus, and called the elders of the church. 28 Take heed therefore unto yourselves, and to all the flock, over the which the Holy Ghost hath made you overseers, to feed the church of God, which he hath purchased with his own blood" Acts 20:17, 28.

Those Elders Of The Church That James Was Referring To Were The Elders Of The Church From Different Congregations.

The Bible said, "14 Is any sick among you? let him call for the elders of the church; and let them pray over him, anointing him with oil in the name of the Lord" James 5:14.

Those Elders Of The Church That Peter Met With; He Ordained Those Elders To Preach The Word Of God.

Peter said, "1 The elders which are among you I exhort, who am also an elder, and a witness of the sufferings of Christ, and also a partaker of the glory that shall be revealed: 2 Feed the flock of God which is among you, taking the oversight thereof, not by constraint, but willingly; not for filthy lucre, but of a ready mind; 3 Neither as being lords over God's heritage, but being ensamples to the flock" 1 Peter 5:1-3.

Paul Charge Timothy And Left Him In Ephesus, And He Told Him To Teach Those Men That Are Teaching, To Teach No Other Doctrine Than That He Had Taught Him.

The Bible said, "1 Paul, an apostle of Jesus Christ by the commandment of God our Saviour, and Lord Jesus Christ, which is our hope; 2 Unto Timothy, my own son in the faith: Grace, mercy, and peace, from God our Father and Jesus Christ our Lord. 3 As I besought thee to abide still at Ephesus, when I went into Macedonia, that thou mightest charge some that they teach no other doctrine, 4 Neither give heed to fables and endless genealogies, which minister questions, rather than godly edifying which is in faith: so do. 7 Desiring to be teachers of the law; understanding neither what they say, nor whereof they affirm" 1 Tim 1:1-4, 7.

Paul said, "1 Thou therefore, my son, be strong in the grace that is in Christ Jesus. 2 And the things that thou hast heard of me among many witnesses, the same commit thou to faithful men, who shall be able to teach others also. 3 Thou therefore endure hardness, as a good soldier of Jesus Christ" 2 Tim 2:1-3.

Paul Taught Timothy That The Man That Desire The Office Of A Bishop, Must Have 17 Qualifications Proven Before He Could Work In That Office. There Is One Qualification That Is Often Overlooked That Paul Taught Timothy; <u>Apt To Teach</u>, Which Mean That That Man Must Be Taught The Duties Of A Bishop.

Paul said, "1 This is a true saying, if a man desire the office of a bishop, he desireth a good work. 2 a bishop then must be (**#1**) blameless, the (**#2**) husband of one wife, (**#3**) vigilant, (**#4**) sober, (**#5**) of good behaviour, (**#6**) given to hospitality, (**#7**) **Apt To Teach**; 3 (**#8**) not given to wine, (**#9**) no striker, (**#10**) not greedy of filthy lucre; (**#11**) but patient, (**#12**) not a brawler, (**#13**) not covetous; 4 (**#14**) one that ruleth well his own house, (**#15**) having his children in subjection with all gravity; 5 (for if a man know not how to rule his own house, how shall he take care of the church of god?) 6 (**#16**) not a novice, lest being lifted up with pride he fall into the condemnation of the devil. 7 (**#17**) moreover he must have a good report of them which are without; lest he fall into reproach and the snare of the devil" 1 Tim 3:1-7.

Paul Taught Timothy Concerning The 8 Qualifications That The Men Must Have That Wanted To Work In The Office Of A Deacon; In Addition He Told Him That Their Wives Must Have 4 Qualifications; Paul Explained To Timothy That Those Qualifications Must Be Proven Before Those Men Could Used The Office Of A Deacon.

Paul said, "8 Likewise must the deacons be (**#1**) grave, (**#2**) not doubletongued, (**#3**) not given to much wine, (**#4**) not greedy of filthy lucre; 9 (**#5**) Holding the mystery of the faith in a pure conscience. 10 And let these also first be proved; then let them use the office of a deacon, (**#6**) being found blameless. 12 (**#7**) Let the deacons be the husbands of one wife, (**#8**) ruling their children and their own houses well. 13 For they that have used the office of a deacon well purchase to themselves a good degree, and great boldness in the faith which is in Christ Jesus" 1 Tim 3:8-10, 12-13.

Paul said, "11 Even so must their wives be (**#1**) grave, (**#2**) not slanderers, **#** (**3**) sober, (**#4**) faithful in all things" 1 Tim 3:11.

Paul Charged Timothy To Preach The Word; But He Did Not Ordain Him An Elder Of The Church.

Paul said, "1 I charge thee therefore before God, and the Lord Jesus Christ, who shall judge the quick and the dead at his appearing and his kingdom; 2 Preach the word; be instant in season, out of season; reprove, rebuke, exhort with all longsuffering and doctrine. 3 For the time will come when they will not endure sound doctrine; but after their own lusts shall they heap to themselves teachers, having itching ears; 4 And they shall turn away their ears from the truth, and shall be turned unto fables" 2 Tim 4:1-4.

Paul Gave Titus A Twofold Mission In Crete, He Told Him To Set In Order The Things That Are Wanting, And Ordain Elders In Every City; And He Gave Titus Nearly The Qualifications That He Gave To Timothy In First Timothy 3:1-7. Which Are The Qualifications Of A Bishop, Paul Pointed Out To Titus, In Titus 1:9 That Those Men Must Be Taught. Let Us Keep In Mind That Paul Did Not Give Titus Any Qualifications That The Elders Must Have Before They Could Be Ordained To Preach The Word.

Paul said, "5 For this cause left I thee in Crete, that thou shouldest set in order the things that are wanting, and ordain elders in every city, as I had appointed thee: 6 (**#1**) if any be blameless, (**#2**) the husband of one wife, (**#3**) having faithful children not accused of riot or unruly. 7 (**#4**) for a bishop must be (**#5**) blameless, as the steward of god; (**#6**) not selfwilled, (**#7**) not soon angry, (**#8**) not given to wine, (**#9**) no striker, (**#10**) not given to filthy lucre; 8 (**#11**) but a lover of hospitality, (**#12**) a lover of good men, (**#13**) sober, (**#14**) just, (**#15**) holy, (**#16**) temperate; 9 (**#17**) holding fast the **faithful word as he hath been taught**, that he may be able by sound doctrine both to exhort and to convince the gainsayers" Titus 1:5-9.

All Christians In The Entire World Should Hold Their Gospel Preachers Accountable Who Are Not Following The Apostles Doctrine, And This Is Obvious Especially In The Case Of Appointing Men To The Office Of A Bishop, To The Position Of A Deacons, And The Position Of The Ordained Elders, In The Church.

The Devil Has Caused Much Confusion In The Church, Concerning The Office Of A Bishop, The Devil Knew That When The Perfect Law Of Liberty Come, That The Position Of The Elders Of The Church Would Cease, So He Influenced His False Writers To Ignore The Word Bishop From; First Timothy 3:1-7, And From Titus 1:5-9. And Replaced It With The Word Elders Of The Church; Which Is Another One Of His False Deceptions, By Which He Have Cause Many Gospel Preachers To Teach Contrary To The Apostles Doctrine, Concerning The Office Of A Bishop, And The Dismantling Of The Position Of Elders Of The Church.

Paul said, "8 Charity never faileth: but whether there be prophecies, they shall fail; whether there be tongues, they shall cease; whether there be knowledge, it shall vanish away. 9 For we know in part, and we prophesy in part. 10 But when that which is perfect is come, then that which is in part shall be done away" 1 Cor 13:8-10.

Before The Perfect Law Of Liberty Came There Is Absolutely No Place In The Scriptures Where The Apostles Ever Mention That The Elders Of The Church Had To Have Any Qualifications Before They Could Be Ordained To Preach The Word Of God.

During The Days Of Pentecost, Those Men That Lead Their Flocks To Jerusalem, Were Elders, The Overseers Of Their Flocks, And After They Were Baptized, They Were Called The Elders Of The Church, And Later On They Were Ordained To Preach The Word Of God.

The Devil Has Caused Many Gospel Preachers To Teach That An Autonomous, Or Independent Congregation Of The Church Cannot Have Just One Ordained Elder Of The Church, They Teach That A Congregation Must Have At Least Two, This Ideology Or Philosophy Is Nothing More Than Another False Doctrine Of The Devil, And These Gospel Preachers Are Going Contrary To The Doctrine Of Christ, Knowing That The Perfect Law Of Liberty Have Come, And Yet They Are Still Ordaining Men With Out The

Authoritative Power Of The Holy Ghost And Calling Them Elders Of The Church.

If All Gospel Preachers Would Rightly Divide The Word Of Truth Concerning The Elders Of The Church, During The Days Of The Apostles, Then They Would Understand That When The Apostles Speak About The Elders Of The Church In The Plural Sense, They Were Not Referring To A Local Congregation Having To Have Multiple Elders, They Were Referring To Elders In Different Congregations, Or In Different Cities.

Some May Say That Those Men That Moses Taught And Set Over The People In Ex 18: Were Elders. Now If That Was True, Then That Would Mean That The Elders Would Have To Be Taught The Qualifications Of Elders Before They Could Be Ordained; Because Moses Taught Those Men, That They Had To Have 3 Qualifications Before They Could Be Appointed To Teach The People.

The Bible said, "17 And Moses' father in law said unto him, The thing that thou doest is not good. 20 And **thou** shalt **teach them ordinances** and **laws**, and shalt **shew them** the way wherein **they must walk**, and the **work** that **they must do**. 21 Moreover thou shalt provide out of all the people **able men**, such as (**1**) fear God, (**2**) men of truth, (**3**) hating covetousness; and place such over them, to be rulers of thousands, and rulers of hundreds, rulers of fifties, and rulers of tens: 24 So Moses hearkened to the voice of his father in law, and did all that he had said" Ex 18:17, 20-21, 24.

According To The Scripture; During The Days Of The Apostles There Were Ordained Elders In Every Church; Or In Every Congregation. Now If That Was Applicable In These Days; That Would Mean That Every Congregation Would Have To Have Elders In Them.

The Bible said, "22 Confirming the souls of the disciples, and exhorting them to continue in the faith, and that we must through much tribulation enter into the kingdom of God. 23 And when they had ordained them elders in every church, and had prayed with fasting, they commended them to the Lord, on whom they believed. 24 And after they had passed throughout Pisidia, they came to Pamphylia" Acts 14:22-24.

If All Believers Would Understand That When Those Evil Theologians Of The Devil Translated The Bible In To Different Languages They Polluted It By Adding And By Taking Away Certain Words And Changing The Meaning Of Them; Intentionally To Cause The Believers To Sin By Believing Their Lies.

John said, "18 For I testify unto every man that heareth the words of the prophecy of this book, If any man shall add unto these things, God shall add unto him the plagues that are written in this book: 19 And if any man shall take away from the words of the book of this prophecy, God shall take away his part out of the book of life, and out of the holy city, and from the things which are written in this book" Rev 22:18-19.

Men And Brethren There Is A Disagreement Among The Churches Of Christ Concerning How Many Men Must Be Over A Congregation Of The Church, This Disagreement Could Be Easily Settle, If All Gospel Preachers Would Speak The Same Thing That John Speak Concerning The Churches Of Christ In Asia.

When The Perfect Law Of Liberty Was Completed; Which Is The Book That We Call The Bible; In The Plural Term John Sent It To The Seven Churches In The Continent Of Asia; Let Us Keep In Mind That When The Church Of Christ Started, Asia Was The Only Continent In The Entire World Where Human Beings Lived.

The Bible said, "10 I was in the Spirit on the Lord's day, and heard behind me a great voice, as of a trumpet, 11 Saying, I am Alpha and Omega, the first and the last: and, What thou seest, write in a book, and send *it* unto the seven churches which are in Asia; **(1)** unto **Ephesus**, **(2)** and unto **Smyrna**, **(3)** and unto **Pergamos**, **(4)** and unto **Thyatira**, **(5)** and unto **Sardis**, **(6)** and unto **Philadelphia**, **(7)** and unto **Laodicea**" Rev 1:10-11.

The Scriptures Further Prove That John Sent That Book To Each Individual Angel Of The Seven Churches In Asia. The Apostle John Absolutely Did Not Send That Book To Two Or More Angels At Each Church.

The Bible said, "1 Unto the **angel** of the **church** (**1**) of **Ephesus** write; 8 And unto the **angel** of the **church** (**2**) in **Smyrna** write; 12 And to the **angel** of the **church** (**3**) in **Pergamos** write; 18 And unto the **angel** of the **church** (**4**) in **Thyatira** write" Rev 2:1, 8, 12, 18.

The Bible said, "1 And unto the **angel** of the **church** (**5**) in **Sardis** write; 7 And to the **angel** of the **church** (**6**) in **Philadelphia** write; 14 And unto the **angel** of the **church** (**7**) of the **Laodiceans** write" Rev 3:1, 7, 14.

Furthermore This Disagreement Would Be Settled If All Christians Would Accept The Reality That Since The Last Apostle Died According To The Scripture, The Ordaining Of The Elders Of The Church Ceased.

During The Days Of The Apostles, They Ordained Elders To Preach The Word Of God; That Being True; Then There Is No Need For A Man Who Have Been Sent To Preach The Word Of God, To Become An Ordained Elder To Preach The Word Of God?

It Would Be Very Helpful Or Conducive To The Future Of The Church, If All Gospel Preachers And Parents Would Teach And Encourage The Young Men To Grow Up In The Church, And To Have A Desire To Become Gospel Preachers, Bishops, And Deacons In The Church.

The Word Elder Is Mention Three Times In First Timothy 5:1-2, 19. And The Word Elders Is Mention One Time In First Timothy 5:17

Now Let Us Keep In Mind That In First Timothy 5:1-2, 17, 19 Paul Was Teaching Timothy To Respect The Older Men And The Older Women.

The Word Elder, Or The Word Elders Was Not Mention Any Other Time In First Timothy, Nor Second Timothy In The KJV Of The Bible, Now This Being True Then Why Does Gospel Preachers Who Claimed To Be Ordaining Elders Of The Church, Refer To First Timothy Chapter Three Where The Word Elder Or Elders Is Not Mention?

Men And Brethren There Is Absolutely No Place In First Or Second Timothy Where Paul Told Timothy To Ordain Elders Of The Church.

Brethren I Truly Believe That When Paul Was Talking To Timothy In First Timothy 1:1 Where He Used The Word Bishop, I Do Not Believe That Paul Made A Mistake And Meant To Say Elder, Because He Used The Word Elder In First Timothy Chapter Five.

All Gospel Preachers Should Know What The Apostle John Said In Revelation 22:18-19 Concerning Adding To And Taking Away From The Word Of God, And Knowing This No Gospel Preacher Should Allow Satan Or Any Other Creature To Cause Them To Deviate From The Word Of God.

John said, "18 And the building of the wall of it was of jasper: and the city was pure gold, like unto clear glass. 19 And the foundations of the wall of the city were garnished with all manner of precious stones. The first foundation was jasper; the second, sapphire; the third, a chalcedony; the fourth, an emerald" Rev 21:18-19.

Plain Talk

Plain Talk Is Making A Conversation Crystal Clear.

Plain Talk Is When A Person Is Talking In Their Native Language To A Foreigner, Who Does Not Understand Their Language, And Then The Person That Is Talking In Their Native Language Began Talking To Them In The Foreigner Native Language, So That The Foreigner Can Understand What They Are Talking About.

On The Day Of Pentecost The Apostles Spoke In Many Different Foreign Languages Through The Power Of The Holy Ghost, And The Foreigners Could Understand Them In Their Native Language.

The Bible said, "1 And when the day of Pentecost was fully come, they were all with one accord in one place. 6 Now when this was noised abroad, the multitude came together, and were confounded, because that every man heard them speak in his own language. 7 And they were all amazed and marvelled, saying one to another, Behold, are not all these which speak Galilaeans? 8 And how hear we every man in our own tongue, wherein we were born?" Acts 2:1, 6-8.

Paul Explained The Church Of Christ In Corinth, That When A Group Of People Come Together In The Church, Speaking In Unknown Tongues (Or In A Foreign Language), And There Be No Interpreter, He Said Let Him Keep Silence In The Church.

Paul said, "2 For he that speaketh in an unknown tongue speaketh not unto men, but unto God: for no man understandeth him; howbeit in the spirit he speaketh mysteries. 4 He that speaketh in an unknown tongue edifieth himself; but he that prophesieth edifieth the church. 5 I would that ye all spake with tongues, but rather that ye prophesied: for greater is he that prophesieth than he that speaketh with tongues, except he interpret, that the church may receive edifying. 9 So likewise ye, except ye utter by the tongue words easy to be understood, how shall it be known what is spoken? for ye shall speak into the air. 28 But if there be no interpreter, let him keep silence in the church; and let him speak to himself, and to God" 1 Cor 14:2, 4-5, 9, 28.

Christ Taught The People In Parables About Seeds That A Man Sowed, And They Ask Him To Tell Them Plainly.

The Bible said, "5 A sower went out to sow his seed: and as he sowed, some fell by the way side; and it was trodden down, and the fowls of the air devoured it. 6 And some fell upon a rock; and as soon as it was sprung up, it withered away, because it lacked moisture. 7 And some fell among thorns; and the thorns sprang up with it, and choked it. 8 And other fell on good ground, and sprang up, and bare fruit an hundredfold. And when he had said these things, he cried, He that hath ears to hear, let him hear. 9 And his disciples asked him, saying, What might this parable be? 10 And he said, Unto you it is given to know the mysteries of the kingdom of God: but to others in parables; that seeing they might not see, and hearing they might not understand" Luke 8:5-10.

Jesus Plainly Made A Promise That He Was Going To Prepare A Place For The Entire World.

Jesus said, "2 In my Father's house are many mansions: if it were not so, I would have told you. I go to prepare a place for you. 3 And if I go and prepare a place for you, I will come again, and receive you unto myself; that where I am, there ye may be also" John 14:2-3.

Jesus Plainly Made A Promise, That Those Who Die In Their Sin Cannot Come To Where He Is.

Jesus said, "21 Then said Jesus again unto them, I go my way, and ye shall seek me, and shall die in your sins: whither I go, ye cannot come. 24 I said therefore unto you, that ye shall die in your sins: for if ye believe not that I am he, ye shall die in your sins" John 8:21, 24.

All Preachers Should Plainly Tell The People That Of All The Religions In The World, There Is Only One Pure Religion.

Paul said, "4 My manner of life from my youth, which was at the first among mine own nation at Jerusalem, know all the Jews; 5 Which knew me from the beginning, if they would testify, that after the most straitest sect of our religion I lived a Pharisee" Acts 26:4-5.

Paul said, "13 For ye have heard of my conversation in time past in the Jews' religion, how that beyond measure I persecuted the church of God, and wasted it: 14 And profited in the Jews' religion above many my equals in mine own nation, being more exceedingly zealous of the traditions of my fathers" Gal 1:13-14.

James said, "26 If any man among you seem to be religious, and bridleth not his tongue, but deceiveth his own heart, this man's religion is vain. 27 Pure religion and undefiled before God and the Father is this, To visit the fatherless and widows in their affliction, and to keep himself unspotted from the world" James 1:26-27.

All Gospel Preachers, Should Plainly Tell The People That There Is Only One Way To Go The Father In Heaven.

The Bible said, "6 Jesus saith unto him, I am the way, the truth, and the life: no man cometh unto the Father, but by me" John 14:6.

All Gospel Preachers Should Plainly Tell The People To Obey God And Prepare Their Souls To Go To Heaven.

Peter said, "17 For the time is come that judgment must begin at the house of God: and if it first begin at us, what shall the end be of them that obey not the gospel of God? 18 And if the righteous scarcely be saved, where shall the ungodly and the sinner appear? 19 Wherefore let them that suffer according to the will of God commit the keeping of their souls to him in well doing, as unto a faithful Creator" 1 Peter 4:17-19.

Christ said, "21 Not every one that saith unto me, Lord, Lord, shall enter into the kingdom of heaven; but he that doeth the will of my Father which is in heaven. 22 Many will say to me in that day, Lord, Lord, have we not prophesied in thy name? and in thy name have cast out devils? and in thy name done many wonderful works? 23 And then will I profess unto them, I never knew you: depart from me, ye that work iniquity" Matt 7:21-23.

Christ said, "28 Come unto me, all ye that labour and are heavy laden, and I will give you rest. 29 Take my yoke upon you, and learn of me; for I am meek and lowly in heart: and ye shall find rest unto your souls.30 For my yoke is easy, and my burden is light" Matt 11:28-30.

John said, "13 And I heard a voice from heaven saying unto me, Write, Blessed are the dead which die in the Lord from henceforth: Yea, saith the Spirit, that they may rest from their labours; and their works do follow them" Rev 14:13.

The Conception, The Birth, And The Death Of Jesus Christ

There Are Seven Questions That I Want To Ask In This Epistle.

1. Where Was The Woman When She Became Conceived, Or Pregnant With Jesus Christ?

John said, "1 And there appeared a great wonder in heaven; a woman clothed with the sun, and the moon under her feet, and upon her head a crown of twelve stars" Rev 12:1.

2. Who Was The Woman That Became Conceived, Or Pregnant, With Jesus Christ?

John said, "14 And to the woman were given two wings of a Great Eagle, that she might fly into the wilderness, into her place, where she is nourished for a time, and times, and half a time, from the face of the serpent" Rev 12:14.

3. Where Was The Mother Of Jesus Christ, When He Was Born?

The Bible said, "4 And Joseph also went up from Galilee, out of the city of Nazareth, into Judaea, unto the city of David, which is called Bethlehem; (because he was of the house and lineage of David:) 5 To be taxed with Mary His Espoused Wife, being great with child. 6 And so it was, that, while they were there, the days were accomplished that she should be delivered. 7 And she brought forth her firstborn son, and wrapped him in swaddling clothes, and laid him in a manger; because there was no room for them in the inn" Luke 2:4-7.

4. What Was The Name Of Jesus Christ Earthly Mother?

The Bible said, "18 Now the birth of Jesus Christ was on this wise: When as his mother Mary was espoused to Joseph, before they came together, she was found with child of the Holy Ghost. 21 And she shall bring forth a son, and thou shalt call his name JESUS: for he shall save his people from their sins" Matt 1:18, 21.

5. Who Truly Was The Mother Of Jesus Christ?

The Bible said, "18 Now the birth of Jesus Christ was on this wise: When as his mother Mary was espoused to Joseph, before they came together, she was found with child of the Holy Ghost. 19 Then Joseph her husband, being a just man, and not willing to make her a publick example, was minded to put her away privily. 20 But while he thought on these things, behold, the angel of the Lord appeared unto him in a dream, saying, Joseph, thou son of David, fear not to take unto thee Mary thy wife: for that which is CONCEIVED in her is of the Holy Ghost. 21 And she shall bring forth a son, and thou shalt call his name JESUS: for he shall save his people from their sins" Matt 1:18-21.

6. What Was Jesus Christ Call After He Was Born?

The Bible said, "23 Behold, a virgin shall be with child, and shall bring forth a son, and they shall call his name Emmanuel, which being interpreted is, God with us" Matt 1:23.

The Bible said, "10 And the angel said unto them, Fear not: for, behold, I bring you good tidings of great joy, which shall be to all people. 11 For unto you is born this day in the city of David a Saviour, which is Christ the Lord" Luke 2:10-11.

The Bible said, "5 So also Christ glorified not himself to be made an high priest; but he that said unto him, Thou art my Son, to day have I begotten thee" Heb 5:5.

The Bible said, "23 Who, when he was reviled, reviled not again; when he suffered, he threatened not; but committed himself to him that judgeth righteously: 24 Who his own self bare our sins in his own body on the tree, that we, being dead to sins, should live unto righteousness: by whose stripes ye were healed. 25 For ye were as sheep going astray; but are now returned unto the Shepherd and Bishop of your souls" 1 Peter 2:23-25.

The Bible said, "16 And he hath on his vesture and on his thigh a name written, KING OF KINGS, AND LORD OF LORDS" Rev 19:16.

7. The Death Of Jesus Christ.

According To The Scripture, Jesus Christ Died in the darkness Between Two Thieves On A Cross.

The Bible said, "33 And when they were come unto a place called Golgotha, that is to say, a place of a skull, 38 Then were there two thieves crucified with him, one on the right hand, and another on the left. 45 Now from the sixth hour there was darkness over all the land unto the ninth hour. 46 And about the ninth hour Jesus cried with a loud voice, saying, Eli, Eli, lama sabachthani? that is to say, My God, my God, why hast thou forsaken me? 50 Jesus, when he had cried again with a loud voice, yielded up the ghost" Matt 27:33, 38, 45-46, 50.

Why People Should Go To The Churches Of Christ

There Are Many Reasons People Should Go To The Church Of Christ.

People Should Go To The Church Of Christ, Because There They Will Learn That It Is Only One Church In The World, And That One Church Is The Church Of Christ.

Christ said, "13 When Jesus came into the coasts of Caesarea Philippi, he asked his disciples, saying, Whom do men say that I the Son of man am? 14 And they said, Some say that thou art John the Baptist: some, Elias; and others, Jeremias, or one of the prophets. 15 He saith unto them, But whom say ye that I am? 16 And Simon Peter answered and said, Thou art the Christ, the Son of the living God. 17 And Jesus answered and said unto him, Blessed art thou, Simon Barjona: for flesh and blood hath not revealed it unto thee, but my Father which is in heaven. 18 And I say also unto thee, That thou art Peter, and upon this rock I will build my church; and the gates of hell shall not prevail against it" Matt 16:13-18.

Christ said, "1 And after six days Jesus taketh Peter, James, and John his brother, and bringeth them up into an high mountain apart, 2 And was transfigured before them: and his face did shine as the sun, and his raiment was white as the light. 3 And, behold, there appeared unto them Moses and Elias talking with him. 4 Then answered Peter, and said unto Jesus, Lord, it is good for us to be here: if thou wilt, let us make here three tabernacles; one for thee, and one for Moses, and one for Elias. 5 While he yet spake, behold, a bright cloud overshadowed them: and behold a voice out of the cloud, which said, This is my beloved Son, in whom I am well pleased; hear ye him" Matt 17:1-5.

People Should Go To The Church Of Christ, To Hear And Learn The Ways Of God.

The Bible said, "3 And many people shall go and say, Come ye, and let us go up to the mountain of the LORD, to the house of the God of Jacob; and he will teach us of his ways, and we will walk in his paths: for out of Zion shall go forth the law, and the word of the LORD from Jerusalem" Isaiah 2:3.

Christ said, "44 No man can come to me, except the Father which hath sent me draw him: and I will raise him up at the last day. 45 It is written in the prophets, And they shall be all taught of God. Every man therefore that hath heard, and hath learned of the Father, cometh unto me" John 6:44-45.

People Should Go To The Church Of Christ, Because There They Can Learn How To Keep The Unclean Spirit From Returning Into Them.

Christ said, "24 When the unclean spirit is gone out of a man, he walketh through dry places, seeking rest; and finding none, he saith, I will return unto my house whence I came out. 25 And when he cometh, he findeth it swept and garnished. 26 Then goeth he, and taketh to him seven other spirits more wicked than himself; and they enter in, and dwell there: and the last state of that man is worse than the first" Luke 11:24-26.

Paul said, "9 Know ye not that the unrighteous shall not inherit the kingdom of God? Be not deceived: neither fornicators, nor idolaters, nor adulterers, nor effeminate, nor abusers of themselves with mankind, 10 Nor thieves, nor covetous, nor drunkards, nor revilers, nor extortioners, shall inherit the kingdom of God. 11 And such were some of you: but ye are washed, but ye are sanctified, but ye are justified in the name of the Lord Jesus, and by the Spirit of our God. 17 Wherefore come out from among them, and be ye separate, saith the Lord, and touch not the unclean thing; and I will receive you, 18 And will be a Father unto you, and ye shall be my sons and daughters, saith the Lord Almighty" 1 Cor 6:9-11, 17-18.

People Should Go To The Church Of Christ, Because There They Can Learn How To Lay Aside Every Weight And Sin.

The Hebrew writer said, "1 Wherefore seeing we also are compassed about with so great a cloud of witnesses, let us lay aside every weight, and the sin which doth so easily beset us, and let us run with patience the race that is set before us, 2 Looking unto Jesus the author and finisher of our faith; who for the joy that was set before him endured the cross, despising the shame, and is set down at the right hand of the throne of God. 3 For consider him that endured such contradiction of sinners against himself, lest ye be wearied and faint in your minds" Heb 12:1-3.

Paul said, "26 Be ye angry, and sin not: let not the sun go down upon your wrath: 27 Neither give place to the devil. 28 Let him that stole steal no more: but rather let him labour, working with his hands the thing which is good, that he may have to give to him that needeth. 29 Let no corrupt communication proceed out of your mouth, but that which is good to the use of edifying, that it may minister grace unto the hearers. 30 And grieve not the holy Spirit of God, whereby ye are sealed unto the day of redemption" Eph 4:26-30.

Paul said, "14 Bless them which persecute you: bless, and curse not. 15 Rejoice with them that do rejoice, and weep with them that weep. 16 Be of the same mind one toward another. Mind not high things, but condescend to men of low estate. Be not wise in your own conceits. 17 Recompense to no man evil for evil. Provide things honest in the sight of all men. 18 If it be possible, as much as lieth in you, live peaceably with all men. 19 Dearly beloved, avenge not yourselves, but rather give place unto wrath: for it is written, Vengeance is mine; I will repay, saith the Lord. 20 Therefore if thine enemy hunger, feed him; if he thirst, give him drink: for in so doing thou shalt heap coals of fire on his head. 21 Be not overcome of evil, but overcome evil with good" Romans 12:14-21.

People Should Go To The Church Of Christ, Because There They Can Learn How To Be Perfect, As God Is Perfect.

Christ said, "48 Be ye therefore perfect, even as your Father which is in heaven is perfect" Matt 5:48.

Paul said, "13 Brethren, I count not myself to have apprehended: but this one thing I do, forgetting those things which are behind, and reaching forth unto those things which are before, 14 I press toward the mark for the prize of the high calling of God in Christ Jesus. 15 Let us therefore, as many as be perfect, be thus minded: and if in any thing ye be otherwise minded, God shall reveal even this unto you. 16 Nevertheless, whereto we have already attained, let us walk by the same rule, let us mind the same thing" Phil 3:13-16.

John said, "16 And we have known and believed the love that God hath to us. God is love; and he that dwelleth in love dwelleth in God, and God in him. 17 Herein is our love made perfect, that we may have boldness in the day of judgment: because as he is, so are we in this world. 18 There is no fear in love; but perfect love casteth out fear: because fear hath torment. He that feareth is not made perfect in love. 19 We love him, because he first loved us" 1 John 4:16-19.

People Should Go To The Churches Of Christ, So That They Can Hear And Obey The Gospel Of Christ, And Remain Faithful To The Church, For The Rest Of Their Lives.

Paul said, "16 Salute one another with an holy kiss. The churches of Christ salute you. 17 Now I beseech you, brethren, mark them which cause divisions and offences contrary to the doctrine which ye have learned; and avoid them" Romans 16:16-17.

David said, "1 The LORD is my shepherd; I shall not want. 2 He maketh me to lie down in green pastures: he leadeth me beside the still waters. 3 He restoreth my soul: he leadeth me in the paths of righteousness for his name's sake. 4 Yea, though I walk through the valley of the shadow of death, I will fear no evil: for thou art with me; thy rod and thy staff they comfort me. 5 Thou preparest a table before me in the presence of mine enemies: thou anointest my head with oil; my cup runneth over. 6 Surely goodness and mercy shall follow me all the days of my life: and I will dwell in the house of the LORD for ever" Psalms 23:1-6.

People Should Go To The Churches Of Christ, To Rejoice And To Be Glad In It.

The Bible said, "1 I was glad when they said unto me, Let us go into the house of the LORD. 2 Our feet shall stand within thy gates, O Jerusalem" Psalms 122:1-2.

The Bible said, "1 Now Peter and John went up together into the temple at the hour of prayer, being the ninth hour. 2 And a certain man lame from his mother's womb was carried, whom they laid daily at the gate of the temple which is called Beautiful, to ask alms of them that entered into the temple; 3 Who seeing Peter and John about to go into the temple asked an alms. 7 And he took him by the right hand, and lifted him up: and immediately his feet and ankle bones received strength. 8 And he leaping up stood, and walked, and entered with them into the temple, walking, and leaping, and praising God. 9 And all the people saw him walking and praising God:" Acts 3:1-3, 7-9.

Who Will Go To Heaven

Those Who Love, And Have Found God, Will Go To Heaven.

The Bible said, "4 Hear, O Israel: The LORD our God is one LORD: 5 And thou shalt love the LORD thy God with all thine heart, and with all thy soul, and with all thy might. 6 And these words, which I command thee this day, shall be in thine heart" Deut 6:4-6.

God said, "17 I love them that love me; and those that seek me early shall find me" Prov 8:17.

Isaiah said, "6 Seek ye the LORD while he may be found, call ye upon him while he is near" Isaiah 55:6.

Paul said, "13 For whosoever shall call upon the name of the Lord shall be saved. 14 How then shall they call on him in whom they have not believed? and how shall they believe in him of whom they have not heard? and how shall they hear without a preacher? 15 And how shall they preach, except they be sent? as it is written, How beautiful are the feet of them that preach the gospel of peace, and bring glad tidings of good things" Romans 10:13-15.

Those Who Seek The Kingdom Of God, And Remain Faithful To The Church Of Christ; Will Go To Heaven.

Daniel said, "44 And in the days of these kings shall the God of heaven set up a kingdom, which shall never be destroyed: and the kingdom shall not be left to other people, *but* it shall break in pieces and consume all these kingdoms, and it shall stand for ever" Dan 2:44.

Christ said, "33 But seek ye first the kingdom of God, and his righteousness; and all these things shall be added unto you" Matt 6:33.

Christ said, "18 And I say also unto thee, That thou art Peter, and upon this rock I will build my church; and the gates of hell shall not prevail against it. 19 And I will give unto thee the keys of the kingdom of heaven: and whatsoever thou shalt bind on earth shall be bound in heaven: and whatsoever thou shalt loose on earth shall be loosed in heaven" Matt 16:18-19.

Paul said, "13 Who hath delivered us from the power of darkness, and hath translated us into the kingdom of his dear Son: 14 In whom we have redemption through his blood, even the forgiveness of sins" Col 1:13-14.

Those Who Have Been Made Clean, And Remain Being Clean; Will Go To Heaven.

Christ said, "3 Now ye are clean through the word which I have spoken unto you. 4 Abide in me, and I in you. As the branch cannot bear fruit of itself, except it abide in the vine; no more can ye, except ye abide in me" John 15:3-4.

Paul said, "25 Husbands, love your wives, even as Christ also loved the church, and gave himself for it; 26 That he might sanctify and cleanse it with the washing of water by the word, 27 That he might present it to himself a glorious church, not having spot, or wrinkle, or any such thing; but that it should be holy and without blemish" Eph 5:25-27.

Those Who Have Obeyed The Gospel Of Christ, And Have Added The Things To Their Faith That Will Keep Them From Falling; Will Go To Heaven.

Peter said, "5 And **beside this**, giving **all diligence**, add to your **faith (1) virtue (desirable quality)**; and to virtue **(2) knowledge (information facts)**; 6 And to knowledge **(3) temperance (self-control)**; and to temperance **(4) patience (staying power)**; and to patience **(5) godliness (holiness)**; 7 And to godliness **(6) brotherly kindness**; and to brotherly kindness **(7) charity (benevolence)**. 8 For if these things be in you, and abound, they make you that ye shall neither be barren nor unfruitful in the knowledge of our Lord Jesus Christ" 2 Peter 1:5-8.

Peter said, "10 Wherefore the rather, brethren, give diligence to make your calling and election sure: for if ye do these things, ye shall never fall: 11 For so an entrance shall be ministered unto you abundantly into the everlasting kingdom of our Lord and Saviour Jesus Christ" 2 Peter 1:10-11.

Those Who Are Following After Righteousness; Will Go To Heaven.

Paul said, "11 But thou, O man of God, flee these things; and follow after righteousness, godliness, faith, love, patience, meekness"1 Tim 6:11.

The Bible said, "34 Then Peter opened his mouth, and said, Of a truth I perceive that God is no respecter of persons: 35 But in every nation he that feareth him, and worketh righteousness, is accepted with him" Acts 10:34-35.

Those Who Are Working For The Lord Until They Die; Will Go To Heaven.

John said, "12 Here is the patience of the saints: here are they that keep the commandments of God, and the faith of Jesus. 13 And I heard a voice from heaven saying unto me, Write, Blessed are the dead which die in the Lord from henceforth: Yea, saith the Spirit, that they may rest from their labours; and their works do follow them" Rev 14:12-13.

Paul said, "13 But I would not have you to be ignorant, brethren, concerning them which are asleep, that ye sorrow not, even as others which have no hope. 14 For if we believe that Jesus died and rose again, even so them also which sleep in Jesus will God bring with him. 15 For this we say unto you by the word of the Lord, that we which are alive and remain unto the coming of the Lord shall not prevent them which are asleep. 16 For the Lord himself shall descend from heaven with a shout, with the voice of the archangel, and with the trump of God: and the dead in Christ shall rise first: 17 Then we which are alive and remain shall be caught up together with them in the clouds, to meet the Lord in the air: and so shall we ever be with the Lord. 18 Wherefore comfort one another with these words" 1 Thess 4:13-18.

Satan And His Dragons

After Satan And His Angles Had Lost The War In Heaven, One Of Satan Dragons Tried To Prevent Christ From Being Born In The Earth.

John said, "1 And there appeared a great wonder in **heaven**; a **woman** clothed with the **sun**, and the **moon** under her **feet**, and upon her **head** a crown of **twelve stars**: 2 And **she being with child cried, travailing** in **birth**, and pained to be **delivered**" Rev 12:1-2.

After Satan And His Dragons Was Cast Out Of Heaven, One Of Them With His Tail Drew Down The Third Part Of The Stars From Heaven.

John said, "3 And there appeared another wonder in heaven; and behold a great red dragon, having seven heads and ten horns, and seven crowns upon his heads. 4 And his tail drew the third part of the stars of heaven, and did cast them to the earth: and the dragon stood before the woman which was ready to be delivered, for to devour her child as soon as it was born. 5 And she brought forth a man child, who was to rule all nations with a rod of iron: and her child was caught up unto God, and to his throne. 6 And the woman fled into the wilderness, where she hath a place prepared of God, that they should feed her there a thousand two hundred and threescore days" Rev 12:3-6.

After Satan And His Angles Was Cast Out Of Heaven, God Told The Earth, And The Sea, That The Devil Is Come Down Unto You.

John said, "10 And I heard a loud voice saying in heaven, Now is come salvation, and strength, and the kingdom of our God, and the power of his Christ: for the accuser of our brethren is cast down, which accused them before our God day and night.12 Therefore rejoice, ye heavens, and ye that dwell in them. Woe to the Inhabiters of the Earth and of the Sea! for the Devil is come down unto you, having Great Wrath, because he knoweth that he hath but a short time. 13 And when the dragon saw that he was cast unto the earth, he persecuted the woman which brought forth the man child. 14 And to the woman were given two wings of a Great Eagle, that she might fly into the wilderness, into her place, where she is nourished for a time, and times, and half a time, from the face of the serpent" Rev 12:10, 12-14.

One Of Satan Dragons Was So Angry Against The Women, That He Sent A Flood Of Water After Her To Destroy Her And Her Unborn Child.

John said, "15 And the serpent cast out of his mouth water as a flood after the woman, that he might cause her to be carried away of the flood. 16 And the earth helped the woman, and the earth opened her mouth, and swallowed up the flood which the dragon cast out of his mouth. 17 And the dragon was wroth with the woman, and went to make war with the remnant of her seed, which keep the commandments of God, and have the testimony of Jesus Christ" Rev 12:15-17.

No Matter How Relentless Satan, And His Dragons Was Against The Woman, And Her Unborned Child, She Still Gave Birth To The Child.

Christ said, "21 And she shall bring forth a son, and thou shalt call his name JESUS: for he shall save his people from their sins. 22 Now all this was done, that it might be fulfilled which was spoken of the Lord by the prophet, saying, 23 Behold, a virgin shall be with child, and shall bring forth a son, and they shall call his name Emmanuel, which being interpreted is, God with us" Matt 1:21-23.

The Bible said, "8 And there were in the same country shepherds abiding in the field, keeping watch over their flock by night. 9 And, lo, the angel of the Lord came upon them, and the glory of the Lord shone round about them: and they were sore afraid. 10 And the angel said unto them, Fear not: for, behold, I bring you good tidings of great joy, which shall be to all people. 11 For unto you is born this day in the city of David a Saviour, which is Christ the Lord" Luke 2:8-11.

After Christ Died, And Was Buried, Satan And His Angles Tried To Keep Christ From Being Raise From The Dead.

The Bible said, "59 And when Joseph had taken the body, he wrapped it in a clean linen cloth, 60 And laid it in his own new tomb, which he had hewn out in the rock: and he rolled a great stone to the door of the sepulchre, and departed. 61 And there was Mary Magdalene, and the other Mary, sitting over against the sepulchre. 62 Now the next day, that followed the day of the preparation, the chief priests and Pharisees came together unto Pilate" Matt 27:59-62,

The Bible said, "63 Saying, Sir, we remember that that deceiver said, while he was yet alive, After three days I will rise again. 64 Command therefore that the sepulchre be made sure until the third day, lest his disciples come by night, and steal him away, and say unto the people, He is risen from the dead: so the last error shall be worse than the first. 65 Pilate said unto them, Ye have a watch: go your way, make it as sure as ye can. 66 So they went, and made the sepulchre sure, sealing the stone, and setting a watch" Matt 27: 63-66.

The Bible said, "1 And when the sabbath was past, Mary Magdalene, and Mary the mother of James, and Salome, had bought sweet spices, that they might come and anoint him. 2 And very early in the morning the first day of the week, they came unto the sepulchre at the rising of the sun. 3 And they said among themselves, Who shall roll us away the stone from the door of the sepulchre? 4 And when they looked, they saw that the stone was rolled away: for it was very great. 5 And entering into the sepulchre, they saw a young man sitting on the right side, clothed in a long white garment; and they were affrighted. 6 And he saith unto them, Be not affrighted: Ye seek Jesus of Nazareth, which was crucified: he is risen; he is not here: behold the place where they laid him. 7 But go your way, tell his disciples and Peter that he goeth before you into Galilee: there shall ye see him, as he said unto you. 8 And they went out quickly, and fled from the sepulchre; for they trembled and were amazed: neither said they any thing to any man; for they were afraid" Mark 16:1-8.

The Bible said, "9 And when he had spoken these things, while they beheld, he was taken up; and a cloud received him out of their sight. 10 And while they looked stedfastly toward heaven as he went up, behold, two men stood by them in white apparel; 11 Which also said, Ye men of Galilee, why stand ye gazing up into heaven? this same Jesus, which is taken up from you into heaven, shall so come in like manner as ye have seen him go into heaven" Acts 1:9-11.

After Christ Rose From The Dead, He Declared That He Was Going To Build His Church, And That All The Power In Hell Can't Stop Him. And He Further Declared That He Had Been Given All Power In Heaven And In Earth.

Christ said, "18 And I say also unto thee, That thou art Peter, and upon this rock I will build my church; and the gates of hell shall not prevail against it" Matt 16:18.

The Bible said, "16 Then the eleven disciples went away into Galilee, into a mountain where Jesus had appointed them. 17 And when they saw him, they worshipped him: but some doubted. 18 And Jesus came and spake unto them, saying, All power is given unto me in heaven and in earth. 19 Go ye therefore, and teach all nations, baptizing them in the name of the Father, and of the Son, and of the Holy Ghost: 20 Teaching them to observe all things whatsoever I have commanded you: and, lo, I am with you alway, even unto the end of the world. Amen" Matt 28:16-20.

After Christ Rose From The Dead, He Conquered The Sting Of Death, And He Conquered The Victory Of The Grave.

The Bible said, "55 O death, where is thy sting? O grave, where is thy victory? 56 The sting of death is sin; and the strength of sin is the law" 1 Cor 15:55-56.

Satan And His Dragons Was So Angry Against God, That After Moses Died, The Devil Himself Tried To Take The Body Of Moses To Hell, But He Could Not.

Jude said, "9 Yet Michael the archangel, when contending with the devil he disputed about the body of Moses, durst not bring against him a railing accusation, but said, The Lord rebuke thee" Jude 1:9.

Doing The Will Of God From The Heart

Human Beings Have Two Hearts; They Have One In Their Chest Which Pumps Blood Through Their Bodies To Sustain Life: The Other Heart Is In Their Head Which Houses The Spirit Of God, This Heart Is Where Wisdom, Knowledge And Understanding Comes From; And This Heart Is Where Christians Worship God From.

Some Time People Will Allow Satan, To Fill Their Hearts To Do Evil Things.

The Bible said, "5 And GOD saw that the wickedness of man was great in the earth, and that every imagination of the thoughts of his heart was only evil continually. 6 And it repented the LORD that he had made man on the earth, and it grieved him at his heart. 7 And the LORD said, I will destroy man whom I have created from the face of the earth; both man, and beast, and the creeping thing, and the fowls of the air; for it repenteth me that I have made them" Gen 6:5-7.

The Bible said, "3 But Peter said, Ananias, why hath Satan filled thine heart to lie to the Holy Ghost, and to keep back part of the price of the land? 4 Whiles it remained, was it not thine own? and after it was sold, was it not in thine own power? why hast thou conceived this thing in thine heart? thou hast not lied unto men, but unto God" Acts 5:3-4.

Jesus Ask Some Of The Scribes, Why Do They Think Evil In Their Hearts.

The Bible said, "2 And, behold, they brought to him a man sick of the palsy, lying on a bed: and Jesus seeing their faith said unto the sick of the palsy; Son, be of good cheer; thy sins be forgiven thee. 3 And, behold, certain of the scribes said within themselves, This man blasphemeth. 4 And Jesus knowing their thoughts said, Wherefore think ye evil in your hearts" Matt 9:2-4.

The Bible Teaches That People Should Do Good Things, From Their Hearts.

Paul said, "6 Not with eyeservice, as menpleasers; but as the servants of Christ, doing the will of God from the heart; 7 With good will doing service, as to the Lord, and not to men" Eph 6:6-7.

Paul said, "14 Bless them which persecute you: bless, and curse not. 15 Rejoice with them that do rejoice, and weep with them that weep. 16 Be of the same mind one toward another. Mind not high things, but condescend to men of low estate. Be not wise in your own conceits. 17 Recompense to no man evil for evil. Provide things honest in the sight of all men. 18 If it be possible, as much as lieth in you, live peaceably with all men. 19 Dearly beloved, avenge not yourselves, but rather give place unto wrath: for it is written, Vengeance is mine; I will repay, saith the Lord. 20 Therefore if thine enemy hunger, feed him; if he thirst, give him drink: for in so doing thou shalt heap coals of fire on his head. 21 Be not overcome of evil, but overcome evil with good" Romans 12:14-21.

Christians Are Taught To Love, And To Serve One Another, With A Pure Heart.

Jesus said, "8 Blessed *are* the pure in heart: for they shall see God" Matt 5:8.

Peter said, "22 Seeing ye have purified your souls in obeying the truth through the Spirit unto unfeigned love of the brethren, see that ye love one another with a pure heart fervently: 23 Being born again, not of corruptible seed, but of incorruptible, by the word of God, which liveth and abideth for ever. 24 For all flesh is as grass, and all the glory of man as the flower of grass. The grass withereth, and the flower thereof falleth away: 25 But the word of the Lord endureth for ever. And this is the word which by the gospel is preached unto you" 1 Peter 1:22-25.

Paul said, "12 Put on therefore, as the elect of God, holy and beloved, bowels of mercies, kindness, humbleness of mind, meekness, longsuffering; 13 Forbearing one another, and forgiving one another, if any man have a quarrel against any: even as Christ forgave you, so also do ye. 14 And above all these things put on charity, which is the bond of perfectness. 15 And let the peace of God rule in your hearts, to the which also ye are called in one body; and be ye thankful. 16 Let the word of Christ dwell in you richly in all wisdom; teaching and admonishing one another in psalms and hymns and spiritual songs, singing with grace in your hearts to the Lord" Col 3:12-16.

Paul said, "15 Unto the pure all things are pure: but unto them that are defiled and unbelieving is nothing pure; but even their mind and conscience is defiled. 16 They profess that they know God; but in works they deny him, being abominable, and disobedient, and unto every good work reprobate" Titus 1:15-16.

Christians Must Make Sure That They Keep Their Hearts Pure, Because They Will Give An Account For Every Idle Word That They Speak In The Judgment.

Jesus said, "36 But I say unto you, That every idle word that men shall speak, they shall give account thereof in the day of judgment. 37 For by thy words thou shalt be justified, and by thy words thou shalt be condemned" Matt 12:36-37.

Paul said, "7 Because the carnal mind is enmity against God: for it is not subject to the law of God, neither indeed can be. 8 So then they that are in the flesh cannot please God. 9 But ye are not in the flesh, but in the Spirit, if so be that the Spirit of God dwell in you. Now if any man have not the Spirit of Christ, he is none of his" Romans 8:7-9.

Paul said, "12 For if there be first a willing mind, *it is* accepted according to that a man hath, *and* not according to that he hath not" 2 Cor 8:12.

Paul said, "5 Let this mind be in you, which was also in Christ Jesus: 6 Who, being in the form of God, thought it not robbery to be equal with God" Phil 2:5-6.

The Hebrew writer said, "17 Obey them that have the rule over you, and submit yourselves: for they watch for your souls, as they that must give account, that they may do it with joy, and not with grief: for that is unprofitable for you. 18 Pray for us: for we trust we have a good conscience, in all things willing to live honestly" Heb 13:17-18.

Peter said, "10 Wherefore the rather, brethren, give diligence to make your calling and election sure: for if ye do these things, ye shall never fall: 11 For so an entrance shall be ministered unto you abundantly into the everlasting kingdom of our Lord and Saviour Jesus Christ" 2 Peter 1:10-11.

Christians Must Never Forget, That They Must Not Let Their Hearts Be Troubled, And They Must Not Let It Be Afraid.

Jesus said, "1 Let not your heart be troubled: ye believe in God, believe also in me. 2 In my Father's house are many mansions: if it were not so, I would have told you. I go to prepare a place for you. 3 And if I go and prepare a place for you, I will come again, and receive you unto myself; that where I am, there ye may be also. 27 Peace I leave with you, my peace I give unto you: not as the world giveth, give I unto you. Let not your heart be troubled, neither let it be afraid" John 14:1-3 27.

Peter said, "5 For this they willingly are ignorant of, that by the word of God the heavens were of old, and the earth standing out of the water and in the water: 6 Whereby the world that then was, being overflowed with water, perished: 7 But the heavens and the earth, which are now, by the same word are kept in store, reserved unto fire against the day of judgment and perdition of ungodly men. 8 But, beloved, be not ignorant of this one thing, that one day is with the Lord as a thousand years, and a thousand years as one day" 2 Peter 3:5-8.

Paul said, "14 And above all these things put on charity, which is the bond of perfectness. 15 And let the peace of God rule in your hearts, to the which also ye are called in one body; and be ye thankful. 16 Let the word of Christ dwell in you richly in all wisdom; teaching and admonishing one another in psalms and hymns and spiritual songs, singing with grace in your hearts to the Lord. 17 And whatsoever ye do in word or deed, do all in the name of the Lord Jesus, giving thanks to God and the Father by him" Col 3:14-17.

Straining At Gnats

A Gnat Is A Small Insect That Pester And Irritate Animals And Human Beings, Causing Them To Lose Sight On What They Were Doing.

In The Spiritual Sense; Gnats Are Described As Some Small Matters, Or Things, That Can Cause People To Lose Sight On Doing The Things That God Have Commanded Them To Do, Causing Them To Lose Their Souls.

Straining At Gnats, Can Cause Blind Guides, And False Preaches To Disguise Themselves As Ministers Of Righteousness, And Cause Those That Follow Them To Lose Their Souls.

Christ said, "24 Ye blind guides, which strain at a gnat, and swallow a camel" Matt 23:24.

Christ said, "15 Beware of false prophets, which come to you in sheep's clothing, but inwardly they are ravening wolves. 16 Ye shall know them by their fruits. Do men gather grapes of thorns, or figs of thistles?" Matt 7:15-16.

Paul said, "13 For such are false apostles, deceitful workers, transforming themselves into the apostles of Christ. 14 And no marvel; for Satan himself is transformed into an angel of light. 15 Therefore it is no great thing if his ministers also be transformed as the ministers of righteousness; whose end shall be according to their works" 2 Cor 11:13-15.

The Bible said, "12 Then came his disciples, and said unto him, Knowest thou that the Pharisees were offended, after they heard this saying? 13 But he answered and said, Every plant, which my heavenly Father hath not planted, shall be rooted up. 14 Let them alone: they be blind leaders of the blind. And if the blind lead the blind, both shall fall into the ditch" Matt 15:12-14.

Straining At Gnats, Can Cause People To Disregard Jesus Truth, And Believe The Devil Lies.

Christ said, "44 Ye are of your father the devil, and the lusts of your father ye will do. He was a murderer from the beginning, and abode not in the truth, because there is no truth in him. When he speaketh a lie, he speaketh of his own: for he is a liar, and the father of it. 45 And because I tell you the truth, ye believe me not" John 8:44-45.

James said, "13 Who is a wise man and endued with knowledge among you? let him shew out of a good conversation his works with meekness of wisdom. 14 But if ye have bitter envying and strife in your hearts, glory not, and lie not against the truth. 15 This wisdom descendeth not from above, but is earthly, sensual, devilish. 16 For where envying and strife is, there is confusion and every evil work" James 3:13-16.

Straining At Gnats, Can Be Dangerous And Detrimental To People Souls, Because It Can Cause God To Send People Strong Delusions, That They Should Believe The Lies Of The Devil, And God Will Damn Those Who Believed Not The Truth, Into Hell With The Devil.

God said, "4 I also will choose their delusions, and will bring their fears upon them; because when I called, none did answer; when I spake, they did not hear: but they did evil before mine eyes, and chose that in which I delighted not" Isaiah 66:4.

The Bible said, "10 And with all deceivableness of unrighteousness in them that perish; because they received not the love of the truth, that they might be saved. 11 And for this cause God shall send them strong delusion, that they should believe a lie: 12 That they all might be damned who believed not the truth, but had pleasure in unrighteousness" 2 Thess 2:10-12.

Peter said, "17 For the time is come that judgment must begin at the house of God: and if it first begin at us, what shall the end be of them that obey not the gospel of God? 18 And if the righteous scarcely be saved, where shall the ungodly and the sinner appear? 19 Wherefore let them that suffer according to the will of God commit the keeping of their souls to him in well doing, as unto a faithful Creator" 1 Peter 4:17-19.

Straining At Gnats, Can Cause Christians To Become Disoriented, Or Confused Concerning Doing One Another The Way That God Commanded Them To Do Toward One Another.

Paul said, "14 Bless them which persecute you: bless, and curse not. 15 Rejoice with them that do rejoice, and weep with them that weep. 16 Be of the same mind one toward another. Mind not high things, but condescend to men of low estate. Be not wise in your own conceits. 17 Recompense to no man evil for evil. Provide things honest in the sight of all men. 18 If it be possible, as much as lieth in you, live peaceably with all men. 19 Dearly beloved, avenge not yourselves, but rather give place unto wrath: for it is written, Vengeance is mine; I will repay, saith the Lord. 20 Therefore if thine enemy hunger, feed him; if he thirst, give him drink: for in so doing thou shalt heap coals of fire on his head. 21 Be not overcome of evil, but overcome evil with good" Romans 12:14-21.

John said, "16 Hereby perceive we the love of God, because he laid down his life for us: and we ought to lay down our lives for the brethren. 17 But whoso hath this world's good, and seeth his brother have need, and shutteth up his bowels of compassion from him, how dwelleth the love of God in him? 18 My little children, let us not love in word, neither in tongue; but in deed and in truth. 19 And hereby we know that we are of the truth, and shall assure our hearts before him" 1 John 3:16-19.

Paul said, "16 Salute one another with an holy kiss. The churches of Christ salute you. 17 Now I beseech you, brethren, mark them which cause divisions and offences contrary to the doctrine which ye have learned; and avoid them. 18 For they that are such serve not our Lord Jesus Christ, but their own belly; and by good words and fair speeches deceive the hearts of the simple" Romans 16:16-18.

Paul said, "11 Finally, brethren, farewell. Be perfect, be of good comfort, be of one mind, live in peace; and the God of love and peace shall be with you. 12 Greet one another with an holy kiss. 13 All the saints salute you. 14 The grace of the Lord Jesus Christ, and the love of God, and the communion of the Holy Ghost, be with you all. Amen" 2 Cor 13:11-14.

Medicine And Physicians

In The Physical Sense, Medicine Is Considered As Drugs, Some Medicines Can Be Administered To Patients Orally, Through The Mouth, And Some Medicines Can Be Administered Intravenously Through The Veins; And Their Doctors Are Call Physicians.

In The Spiritual Sense, Medicine Is The Healing Power Of The Word Of God; And It Is Administered Through The Ears To The Hearts Of Mankind Through The Preaching Of Gospel Preachers; Who Are The Physicians Of God, And The Healing Comes Through Faith.

Paul said, "17 So then faith cometh by hearing, and hearing by the word of God" Romans 10:17.

The Bible Teach That People Can Get The Things That They Need From God Through Faith, And Hope.

The Hebrew Writer Said, 1 Now faith is the substance of things hoped for, the evidence of things not seen" Heb 11:1.

James Made It Crystal Clear, That Faith In The Word Of God Is No Good Without Works.

James said, "22 Seest thou how faith wrought with his works, and by works was faith made perfect? 23 And the scripture was fulfilled which saith, Abraham believed God, and it was imputed unto him for righteousness: and he was called the Friend of God. 24 Ye see then how that by works a man is justified, and not by faith only. 25 Likewise also was not Rahab the harlot justified by works, when she had received the messengers, and had sent them out another way? 26 For as the body without the spirit is dead, so faith without works is dead also" James 2:22-26.

The Bible Said, That In The Old Time God Ask, Was There No Medicine, Nor Physicians In Gilead?

Jeremiah said, "20 The harvest is past, the summer is ended, and we are not saved. 21 For the hurt of the daughter of my people am I hurt; I am black; astonishment hath taken hold on me. 22 Is there no balm (Medicine) in Gilead; is there no physician there? why then is not the health of the daughter of my people recovered?" Jer 8:20-22.

The Bible Teach That The Spiritual Medicine, Is Administered To Those Who Walk In The Counsel Of God.

David said, "1 Blessed is the man that walketh not in the counsel of the ungodly, nor standeth in the way of sinners, nor sitteth in the seat of the scornful. 2 But his delight is in the law of the LORD; and in his law doth he meditate day and night. 3 And he shall be like a tree planted by the rivers of water, that bringeth forth his fruit in his season; his leaf also shall not wither; and whatsoever he doeth shall prosper. 4 The ungodly are not so: but are like the chaff which the wind driveth away. 5 Therefore the ungodly shall not stand in the judgment, nor sinners in the congregation of the righteous. 6 For the LORD knoweth the way of the righteous: but the way of the ungodly shall perish" Psalms 1:1-6.

Ezekiel said, "12 And by the river upon the bank thereof, on this side and on that side, shall grow all trees for meat, whose leaf shall not fade, neither shall the fruit thereof be consumed: it shall bring forth new fruit according to his months, because their waters they issued out of the sanctuary: and the fruit thereof shall be for meat, and the leaf thereof for medicine" Ezek 47:12.

John said, "1 And he shewed me a pure river of water of life, clear as crystal, proceeding out of the throne of God and of the Lamb. 2 In the midst of the street of it, and on either side of the river, was there the tree of life, which bare twelve manner of fruits, and yielded her fruit every month: and the leaves of the tree were for the healing of the nations. 3 And there shall be no more curse: but the throne of God and of the Lamb shall be in it; and his servants shall serve him" Rev 22:1-3.

The Bible Teach, That The Spiritual Medicine Work In Those Who Believe, And Trust In The Lord.

Solomon said, "5 Trust in the LORD with all thine heart; and lean not unto thine own understanding. 6 In all thy ways acknowledge him, and he shall direct thy paths. 7 Be not wise in thine own eyes: fear the LORD, and depart from evil. 8 It shall be health to thy navel, and marrow to thy bones" Prov 3:5-8.

The Bible Teach, That When Naaman Believed And Trusted In The Lord, Then He Was Made Clean.

The Bible said, "1 Now Naaman, captain of the host of the king of Syria, was a great man with his master, and honourable, because by him the LORD had given deliverance unto Syria: he was also a mighty man in valour, but he was a leper. 3 And she said unto her mistress, Would God my lord were with the prophet that is in Samaria! for he would recover him of his leprosy" 2 Kings 5:1,3.

The Bible said, "13 And his servants came near, and spake unto him, and said, My father, if the prophet had bid thee do some great thing, wouldest thou not have done it? how much rather then, when he saith to thee, Wash, and be clean? 14 Then went he down, and dipped himself seven times in Jordan, according to the saying of the man of God: and his flesh came again like unto the flesh of a little child, and he was clean" 2 Kings 5:13-14.

The Bible Teach, That Hezekiah Believed, And Trusted In The Lord, And He Was Made Well.

The Bible said, "1 In those days was Hezekiah sick unto death. And Isaiah the prophet the son of Amoz came unto him, and said unto him, Thus saith the LORD, Set thine house in order: for thou shalt die, and not live. 2 Then Hezekiah turned his face toward the wall, and prayed unto the LORD, 3 And said, Remember now, O LORD, I beseech thee, how I have walked before thee in truth and with a perfect heart, and have done that which is good in thy sight. And Hezekiah wept sore. 4 Then came the word of the LORD to Isaiah, saying, 5 Go, and say to Hezekiah, Thus saith the LORD, the God of David thy father, I have heard thy prayer, I have seen thy tears: behold, I will add unto thy days fifteen years" Isaiah 38:1-5.

The Bible Teach, That The Centurion That Came To Jesus, Believed, And Trusted In The Lord, And His Servant Was Healed.

Jesus said, "5 And when Jesus was entered into Capernaum, there came unto him a centurion, beseeching him, 6 And saying, Lord, my servant lieth at home sick of the palsy, grievously tormented. 7 And Jesus saith unto him, I will come and heal him. 8 The centurion answered and said, Lord, I am not worthy that thou shouldest come under my roof: but speak the word only, and my servant shall be healed. 13 And Jesus said unto the centurion, Go thy way; and as thou hast believed, so be it done unto thee. And his servant was healed in the selfsame hour" Matt 8:5-8, 13.

The Bible Teach That The Father Who's Son Had A Dumb And Deaf Spirit, Believed, And Trusted In The Lord, And His Son Was Made Well.

Jesus said, "17 And one of the multitude answered and said, Master, I have brought unto thee my son, which hath a dumb spirit; 23 Jesus said unto him, If thou canst believe, all things are possible to him that believeth. 24 And straightway the father of the child cried out, and said with tears, Lord, I believe; help thou mine unbelief. 25 When Jesus saw that the people came running together, he rebuked the foul spirit, saying unto him, Thou dumb and deaf spirit, I charge thee, come out of him, and enter no more into him. 26 And the spirit cried, and rent him sore, and came out of him: and he was as one dead; insomuch that many said, He is dead. 27 But Jesus took him by the hand, and lifted him up; and he arose" Mark 9:17, 23-27.

The Bible Teach, That The Woman With The Issue Of Blood, Believed, And Trusted In The Lord, And She Was Made Whole.

The Bible said, '43 And a woman having an issue of blood twelve years, which had spent all her living upon physicians, neither could be healed of any, 44 Came behind him, and touched the border of his garment: and immediately her issue of blood stanched. 47 And when the woman saw that she was not hid, she came trembling, and falling down before him, she declared unto him before all the people for what cause she had touched him, and how she was healed immediately. 48 And he said unto her, Daughter, be of good comfort: thy faith hath made thee whole; go in peace" Luke 8:43-44, 47-48.

The Bible Teach, That The Nobleman That Came To Jesus Believed, And Trusted In The Lord, And His Son Was Made Well.

John said, "49 The nobleman saith unto him, Sir, come down ere my child die. 50 Jesus saith unto him, Go thy way; thy son liveth. And the man believed the word that Jesus had spoken unto him, and he went his way. 51 And as he was now going down, his servants met him, and told him, saying, Thy son liveth. 52 Then enquired he of them the hour when he began to amend. And they said unto him, Yesterday at the seventh hour the fever left him. 53 So the father knew that it was at the same hour, in the which Jesus said unto him, Thy son liveth: and himself believed, and his whole house. 54 This is again the second miracle that Jesus did, when he was come out of Judaea into Galilee" John 4:49-54.

The Bible Teach, That The Man That Was Paralyzed At Pool Of Bethesda, Believed, And Trusted In The Lord, And He Was Made Whole.

The Bible said, "2 Now there is at Jerusalem by the sheep market a pool, which is called in the Hebrew tongue Bethesda, having five porches. 3 In these lay a great multitude of impotent folk, of blind, halt, withered, waiting for the moving of the water. 8 Jesus saith unto him, Rise, take up thy bed, and walk. 9 And immediately the man was made whole, and took up his bed, and walked: and on the same day was the sabbath. 10 The Jews therefore said unto him that was cured, It is the sabbath day: it is not lawful for thee to carry thy bed. 11 He answered them, He that made me whole, the same said unto me, Take up thy bed, and walk" John 5:2-3, 8-11.

The Bible Teach, That The Sick Christians That Believed, And Trusted In The Lord, That They Will Be Healed.

James said, "13 Is any among you afflicted? let him pray. Is any merry? let him sing psalms. 14 Is any sick among you? let him call for the elders of the church; and let them pray over him, anointing him with oil in the name of the Lord: 15 And the prayer of faith shall save the sick, and the Lord shall raise him up; and if he have committed sins, they shall be forgiven him. 16 Confess your faults one to another, and pray one for another, that ye may be healed. The effectual fervent prayer of a righteous man availeth much" James 5:13-16.

The Bible Teach, That Those Who Believed, And Trusted In The Lord, And Have Joy In Their Heart, Shell Receive The Medicine Of God To Keep Them Whole.

Solomon said, "22 A merry heart doeth good like a medicine: but a broken spirit drieth the bones" Prov 17:22.

John said, "11 These things have I spoken unto you, that my joy might remain in you, and that your joy might be full. 12 This is my commandment, That ye love one another, as I have loved you. 13 Greater love hath no man than this, that a man lay down his life for his friends. 14 Ye are my friends, if ye do whatsoever I command you" John 15:11-14.

The Bible Teach, That There Are Many Preachers That Cannot Profit The People At All.

Job said, "4 But ye *are* forgers of lies, ye *are* all physicians of no value" Job 13:4.

Jeremiah said, "32 Behold, I *am* against them that prophesy false dreams, saith the LORD, and do tell them, and cause my people to err by their lies, and by their lightness; yet I sent them not, nor commanded them: therefore they shall not profit this people at all, saith the LORD" Jer 23:32.

The Bible said, "25 And a certain woman, which had an issue of blood twelve years, 26 And had suffered many things of many physicians, and had spent all that she had, and was nothing bettered, but rather grew worse" Mark 5:25-26.

No Time

The Statement No Time Is A Phrase That Means, That Time Is No Longer.

According To The Bible There Is A Time For Every Thing.

Solomon said, "1 To every thing there is a season, and a time to every purpose under the heaven: 2 A time to be born, and a time to die; a time to plant, and a time to pluck up that which is planted; 3 A time to kill, and a time to heal; a time to break down, and a time to build up; 4 A time to weep, and a time to laugh; a time to mourn, and a time to dance; 5 A time to cast away stones, and a time to gather stones together; a time to embrace, and a time to refrain from embracing; 6 A time to get, and a time to lose; a time to keep, and a time to cast away; 7 A time to rend, and a time to sew; a time to keep silence, and a time to speak; 8 A time to love, and a time to hate; a time of war, and a time of peace" Eccl 3:1-8.

Paul said, "1 We then, as workers together with him, beseech you also that ye receive not the grace of God in vain. 2 For he saith, I have heard thee in a time accepted, and in the day of salvation have I succoured thee: behold, now is the accepted time; behold, now is the day of salvation" 2 Cor 6:1-2.

Some People May Say; I Kneel To Pray But Not For Long, I Have Too Much To Do, I Must Hurry Off And Get To Work, Because Bills Will Soon Be Due.

Solomon said, "10 Whatsoever thy hand findeth to do, do *it* with thy might; for *there is* no work, nor device, nor knowledge, nor wisdom, in the grave, whither thou goest" Eccl 9:10.

Jesus said, "6 But thou, when thou prayest, enter into thy closet, and when thou hast shut thy door, pray to thy Father which is in secret; and thy Father which seeth in secret shall reward thee openly. 7 But when ye pray, use not vain repetitions, as the heathen do: for they think that they shall be heard for their much speaking. 34 Take therefore no thought for the morrow: for the morrow shall take thought for the things of itself. Sufficient unto the day is the evil thereof" Matt 6:6-7, 34.

Paul said, "12 Wherefore, my beloved, as ye have always obeyed, not as in my presence only, but now much more in my absence, work out your own salvation with fear and trembling. 13 For it is God which worketh in you both to will and to do of his good pleasure" Phil 2:12-13.

Some People May Say: I Said A Hurried Prayer, Jumped Up From Off Of My Knees, And Said To Myself, My Christian Duties Are Now Done, My Soul Can Be At Ease.

The Bible said, "30 And Jesus answering said, A certain man went down from Jerusalem to Jericho, and fell among thieves, which stripped him of his raiment, and wounded him, and departed, leaving him half dead. 31 And by chance there came down a certain priest that way: and when he saw him, he passed by on the other side. 32 And likewise a Levite, when he was at the place, came and looked on him, and passed by on the other side. 33 But a certain Samaritan, as he journeyed, came where he was: and when he saw him, he had compassion on him, 34 And went to him, and bound up his wounds, pouring in oil and wine, and set him on his own beast, and brought him to an inn, and took care of him" Luke 10:30-34.

The Bible said, "16 And he spake a parable unto them, saying, The ground of a certain rich man brought forth plentifully: 17 And he thought within himself, saying, What shall I do, because I have no room where to bestow my fruits? 18 And he said, This will I do: I will pull down my barns, and build greater; and there will I bestow all my fruits and my goods. 19 And I will say to my soul, Soul, thou hast much goods laid up for many years; take thine ease, eat, drink, and be merry. 20 But God said unto him, Thou fool, this night thy soul shall be required of thee: then whose shall those things be, which thou hast provided? 21 So is he that layeth up treasure for himself, and is not rich toward God" Luke 12:16-21.

Jude said, "21 Keep yourselves in the love of God, looking for the mercy of our Lord Jesus Christ unto eternal life. 22 And of some have compassion, making a difference: 23 And others save with fear, pulling them out of the fire; hating even the garment spotted by the flesh. 24 Now unto him that is able to keep you from falling, and to present you faultless before the presence of his glory with exceeding joy, 25 To the only wise God our Saviour, be glory and majesty, dominion and power, both now and ever. Amen" Jude 1:21-25.

Some People May Say: I Go All Through The Day, And I Have No Time To Speak A Word Of Cheer, I Have No Time To Speak Of Christ To Friends, And People That I Know To Me That They Are Dear.

Solomon said, "17 A friend loveth at all times, and a brother is born for adversity. 18 A man void of understanding striketh hands, and becometh surety in the presence of his friend. 19 He loveth transgression that loveth strife: and he that exalteth his gate seeketh destruction" Prov 17:17-19.

The Bible said, '5 And he said unto them, Which of you shall have a friend, and shall go unto him at midnight, and say unto him, Friend, lend me three loaves; 6 For a friend of mine in his journey is come to me, and I have nothing to set before him? 7 And he from within shall answer and say, Trouble me not: the door is now shut, and my children are with me in bed; I cannot rise and give thee" Luke 11:5-7.

Jesus said, "14 Ye are my friends, if ye do whatsoever I command you. 15 Henceforth I call you not servants; for the servant knoweth not what his lord doeth: but I have called you friends; for all things that I have heard of my Father I have made known unto you" John 15:14-15.

Some People May Say; I Have No Time, No Time, Too Much To Do, And That Is Their Constant Cry, No Time To Give To Those In Need.

John said, "17 But whoso hath this world's good, and seeth his brother have need, and shutteth up his bowels of compassion from him, how dwelleth the love of God in him? 18 My little children, let us not love in word, neither in tongue; but in deed and in truth. 19 And hereby we know that we are of the truth, and shall assure our hearts before him. 20 For if our heart condemn us, God is greater than our heart, and knoweth all things. 21 Beloved, if our heart condemn us not, then have we confidence toward God" 1 John 3:17-21.

The Bible said, "20 And there was a certain beggar named Lazarus, which was laid at his gate, full of sores, 21 And desiring to be fed with the crumbs which fell from the rich man's table: moreover the dogs came and licked his sores" Luke 16:20-21.

What Will Some People Do After It Come Their Time To Die, Will They Stand Before The Lord In The Day Of Judgment With Down Cast Eyes, Will They See Within His Hands The Book Of Life, Will They Be Wondering When He Open The Book, Will He Find Their Names Written In Side, Or Will They Be Wondering, Did They Ever Obey The Gospel Of Christ Before They Died, Or Did They Ever Find The Time?

Jesus said, "21 Then said Jesus again unto them, I go my way, and ye shall seek me, and shall die in your sins: whither I go, ye cannot come. 22 Then said the Jews, Will he kill himself? because he saith, Whither I go, ye cannot come. 24 I said therefore unto you, that ye shall die in your sins: for if ye believe not that I am he, ye shall die in your sins" John 8:21-22, 24.

The Hebrew writer said, "27 And as it is appointed unto men once to die, but after this the judgment: 28 So Christ was once offered to bear the sins of many; and unto them that look for him shall he appear the second time without sin unto salvation" Heb 9:27-28.

John said, "5 He that overcometh, the same shall be clothed in white raiment; and I will not blot out his name out of the book of life, but I will confess his name before my Father, and before his angels. 6 He that hath an ear, let him hear what the Spirit saith unto the churches" Rev 3:5-6.

John said, "1 And I stood upon the sand of the sea, and saw a beast rise up out of the sea, having seven heads and ten horns, and upon his horns ten crowns, and upon his heads the name of blasphemy. 2 And the beast which I saw was like unto a leopard, and his feet were as the feet of a bear, and his mouth as the mouth of a lion: and the dragon gave him his power, and his seat, and great authority. 8 And all that dwell upon the earth shall worship him, whose names are not written in the book of life of the Lamb slain from the foundation of the world" Rev 13:1-2, 8.

John said, "13 And I heard a voice from heaven saying unto me, Write, Blessed *are* the dead which die in the Lord from henceforth: Yea, saith the Spirit, that they may rest from their labours; and their works do follow them" Rev 14:13.

Paul said, "24 Then cometh the end, when he shall have delivered up the kingdom to God, even the Father; when he shall have put down all rule and all authority and power. 25 For he must reign, till he hath put all enemies under his feet. 26 The last enemy that shall be destroyed is death" 1 Cor 15:24-26.

John said, "15 And the kings of the earth, and the great men, and the rich men, and the chief captains, and the mighty men, and every bondman, and every free man, hid themselves in the dens and in the rocks of the mountains; 16 And said to the mountains and rocks, Fall on us, and hide us from the face of him that sitteth on the throne, and from the wrath of the Lamb: 17 For the great day of his wrath is come; and who shall be able to stand?" Rev 6:15-17.

The World

When God Created The Heaven And The Earth, The Earth Was Full Of Water, And The Spirit Of God Separated The Water From The Earth, And The Dry Land Appeared, And The Dry Land Was Call Earth Or World.

The Bible said, "1 In the beginning God created the heaven and the **earth**. 2 And the earth was without form, and void; and darkness was upon the face of the deep. And the Spirit of God moved upon the face of the waters. 3 And God said, Let there be light: and there was light. 4 And God saw the light, that it was good: and God divided the light from the darkness. 5 And God called the light Day, and the darkness he called Night. And the evening and the morning were the first day" Gen 1:1-5.

The Bible said, "9 And God said, Let the waters under the heaven be gathered together unto one place, and let the dry land appear: and it was so. 10 And God called the dry land **Earth**; and the gathering together of the waters called he Seas: and God saw that it was good. 11 And God said, Let the earth bring forth grass, the herb yielding seed, and the fruit tree yielding fruit after his kind, whose seed is in itself, upon the earth: and it was so. 12 And the earth brought forth grass, and herb yielding seed after his kind, and the tree yielding fruit, whose seed was in itself, after his kind: and God saw that it was good" Gen 1:9-12.

Samuel said, "8 He raiseth up the poor out of the dust, and lifteth up the beggar from the dunghill, to set them among princes, and to make them inherit the throne of glory: for the pillars of the earth are the LORD'S, and he hath set the **world** upon them. 9 He will keep the feet of his saints, and the wicked shall be silent in darkness; for by strength shall no man prevail" 1 Sam 2:8-9.

After God Made Man In The Earth, And Gave Him Everything That He Need To Sustain In The World, Yet Man Allowed His Heart To Become Wicked, In The Sight Of God.

The Bible said, "5 And GOD saw that the wickedness of man was great in the earth, and that every imagination of the thoughts of his heart was only evil continually. 6 And it repented the LORD that he had made man on the earth, and it grieved him at his heart. 7 And the LORD said, I will destroy man whom I have created from the face of the earth; both man, and beast, and the creeping thing, and the fowls of the air; for it repenteth me that I have made them" Gen 6:5-7.

A Group Of Homosexuals, Came To Lot's House And Demanded That He Send Those Men That Was In His House, Out To Them So That They May Know Them; Which Mean So That They Can Rape Them.

The Bible said, "1 And there came two angels to Sodom at even; and Lot sat in the gate of Sodom: and Lot seeing them rose up to meet them; and he bowed himself with his face toward the ground; 2 And he said, Behold now, my lords, turn in, I pray you, into your servant's house, and tarry all night, and wash your feet, and ye shall rise up early, and go on your ways. And they said, Nay; but we will abide in the street all night. 3 And he pressed upon them greatly; and they turned in unto him, and entered into his house; and he made them a feast, and did bake unleavened bread, and they did eat" Gen 19:1-3.

The Bible said, "4 But before they lay down, the men of the city, even the men of Sodom, compassed the house round, both old and young, all the people from every quarter: 5 And they called unto Lot, and said unto him, Where are the men which came in to thee this night? bring them out unto us, that we may know them. 6 And Lot went out at the door unto them, and shut the door after him, 7 And said, I pray you, brethren, do not so wickedly" Gen 19:4-7.

Lot Pleaded With Those Homosexuals Men, To Leave Those Men Alone, And Take His Two Virgin's **Daughters Instead, But Those Men Refused, And Demanded That He Send Those Men Out To Them.**

The Bible said, "8 Behold now, I have two daughters which have not known man; let me, I pray you, bring them out unto you, and do ye to them as is good in your eyes: only unto these men do nothing; for therefore came they under the shadow of my roof. 9 And they said, Stand back. And they said again, This one fellow came in to sojourn, and he will needs be a judge: now will we deal worse with thee, than with them. And they pressed sore upon the man, even Lot, and came near to break the door" Gen 19:8-9.

Paul Warned The Christians In Rome, About Them Turning Back To Their Old Ways, And He Informed Them That God Was Going To Hold Them Accountable For Their Sins.

Paul said, "18 For the wrath of God is revealed from heaven against all ungodliness and unrighteousness of men, who hold the truth in unrighteousness; 19 Because that which may be known of God is manifest in them; for God hath shewed it unto them. 20 For the invisible things of him from the creation of the world are clearly seen, being understood by the things that are made, even his eternal power and Godhead; so that they are without excuse: 21 Because that, when they knew God, they glorified him not as God, neither were thankful; but became vain in their imaginations, and their foolish heart was darkened" Romans 1:18-21.

The Bible said, "22 Professing themselves to be wise, they became fools, 23 And changed the glory of the uncorruptible God into an image made like to corruptible man, and to birds, and fourfooted beasts, and creeping things. 24 Wherefore God also gave them up to uncleanness through the lusts of their own hearts, to dishonour their own bodies between themselves: 25 Who changed the truth of God into a lie, and worshipped and served the creature more than the Creator, who is blessed for ever. Amen" Romans 1:22-25.

The Bible said, "26 For this cause God gave them up unto vile affections: for even their women did change the natural use into that which is against nature: 27 And likewise also the men, leaving the natural use of the woman, burned in their lust one toward another; men with men working that which is unseemly, and receiving in themselves that recompence of their error which was meet" Romans 1:26-27.

Paul said, "28 And even as they did not like to retain God in their knowledge, God gave them over to a reprobate mind, to do those things which are not convenient; 29 Being filled with all unrighteousness, fornication, wickedness, covetousness, maliciousness; full of envy, murder, debate, deceit, malignity; whisperers, 30 Backbiters, haters of God, despiteful, proud, boasters, inventors of evil things, disobedient to parents, 31 Without understanding, covenantbreakers, without natural affection, implacable, unmerciful: 32 Who knowing the judgment of God, that they which commit such things are worthy of death, not only do the same, but have pleasure in them that do them Romans" 1:28-32.

Paul Gave The Christians In Corinth, A Warning From God, To Flee From Those Who Are Living Immoral Lives, And He Told Them To Remain Being Faithful Unto Him.

Paul said, "11 O ye Corinthians, our mouth is open unto you, our heart is enlarged. 12 Ye are not straitened in us, but ye are straitened in your own bowels. 13 Now for a recompence in the same, (I speak as unto my children,) be ye also enlarged. 14 Be ye not unequally yoked together with unbelievers: for what fellowship hath righteousness with unrighteousness? and what communion hath light with darkness? 15 And what concord hath Christ with Belial? or what part hath he that believeth with an infidel?" 2 Cor 6:11-15

Paul said, "16 And what agreement hath the temple of God with idols? for ye are the temple of the living God; as God hath said, I will dwell in them, and walk in them; and I will be their God, and they shall be my people. 17 Wherefore come out from among them, and be ye separate, saith the Lord, and touch not the unclean thing; and I will receive you, 18 And will be a Father unto you, and ye shall be my sons and daughters, saith the Lord Almighty" 2 Cor 6:16-18.

Jesus Christ Gave Warning, To The Entire World, To Get And Stay Prepared To Meet Him Before He Come, And The Door Be Shut.

The Bible said, "1 Then shall the kingdom of heaven be likened unto ten virgins, which took their lamps, and went forth to meet the bridegroom. 2 And five of them were wise, and five were foolish. 3 They that were foolish took their lamps, and took no oil with them: 6 And at midnight there was a cry made, Behold, the bridegroom cometh; go ye out to meet him. 7 Then all those virgins arose, and trimmed their lamps. 8 And the foolish said unto the wise, Give us of your oil; for our lamps are gone out. 9 But the wise answered, saying, Not so; lest there be not enough for us and you: but go ye rather to them that sell, and buy for yourselves" Matt 25:1-3, 6-9.

The Bible said, "10 And while they went to buy, the bridegroom came; and they that were ready went in with him to the marriage: and the door was shut. 11 Afterward came also the other virgins, saying, Lord, Lord, open to us. 12 But he answered and said, Verily I say unto you, I know you not. 13 Watch therefore, for ye know neither the day nor the hour wherein the Son of man cometh" Matt 25:10-13.

James Gave Warning, To The Entire World To Stop Sinning, And Obey The Word Of God, Before It Is Too Late.

James said, "21 Wherefore lay apart all filthiness and superfluity of naughtiness, and receive with meekness the engrafted word, which is able to save your souls. 22 But be ye doers of the word, and not hearers only, deceiving your own selves. 23 For if any be a hearer of the word, and not a doer, he is like unto a man beholding his natural face in a glass: 24 For he beholdeth himself, and goeth his way, and straightway forgetteth what manner of man he was. 25 But whoso looketh into the perfect law of liberty, and continueth therein, he being not a forgetful hearer, but a doer of the work, this man shall be blessed in his deed" James 1:21-25.

Nahum said, "3 The LORD is slow to anger, and great in power, and will not at all acquit the wicked: the LORD hath his way in the whirlwind and in the storm, and the clouds are the dust of his feet. 4 He rebuketh the sea, and maketh it dry, and drieth up all the rivers: Bashan languisheth, and Carmel, and the flower of Lebanon languisheth. 5 The mountains quake at him, and the hills melt, and the earth is burned at his presence, yea, the world, and all that dwell therein. 6 Who can stand before his indignation? and who can abide in the fierceness of his anger? his fury is poured out like fire, and the rocks are thrown down by him. 7 The LORD is good, a strong hold in the day of trouble; and he knoweth them that trust in him. 8 But with an overrunning flood he will make an utter end of the place thereof, and darkness shall pursue his enemies" Nahum 1:3-8.

The Earth, And The World That God Created In The Beginning, He Will Destroy In The End.

Peter said, "10 But the day of the Lord will come as a thief in the night; in the which the heavens shall pass away with a great noise, and the elements shall melt with fervent heat, the earth also and the works that are therein shall be burned up. 11 Seeing then that all these things shall be dissolved, what manner of persons ought ye to be in all holy conversation and godliness, 12 Looking for and hasting unto the coming of the day of God, wherein the heavens being on fire shall be dissolved, and the elements shall melt with fervent heat? 13 Nevertheless we, according to his promise, look for new heavens and a new earth, wherein dwelleth righteousness. 14 Wherefore, beloved, seeing that ye look for such things, be diligent that ye may be found of him in peace, without spot, and blameless" 2 Peter 3:10-14.

Job Went Through Lots Of Chaos And Troubles While Living In The World, Yet He Remains Being A Perfect And Upright Man, He Refused To Allow Satan; Or His Friends To Destroy His Faith In God; And He Maintained His Integrity.

The Bible said, "1 There was a man in the land of Uz, whose name was Job; and that man was perfect and upright, and one that feared God, and eschewed evil" Job 1:1.

The Bible said, "3 And the LORD said unto Satan, Hast thou considered my servant Job, that there is none like him in the earth, a perfect and an upright man, one that feareth God, and escheweth evil? and still he holdeth fast his integrity, although thou movedst me against him, to destroy him without cause" Job 2:3.

The Bible said, "9 Then said his wife unto him, Dost thou still retain thine integrity? curse God, and die" Job 2:9.

The Bible said, "5 God forbid that I should justify you: till I die I will not remove mine integrity from me. 6 My righteousness I hold fast, and will not let it go: my heart shall not reproach me so long as I live" Job 27:5-6.

The Bible said, "15 Though he slay me, yet will I trust in him: but I will maintain mine own ways before him" Job 13:15.

Preaching To Save Souls; Or Preaching For A Living

Gospel Preachers Are To Preach The Gospel Of Christ, Hoping To Save People Souls.

Jeremiah Did Not Preach For Money, He Preached To Save The People Souls, And He Did It Sincerely.

Jeremiah said, "7 O LORD, thou hast deceived me, and I was deceived: thou art stronger than I, and hast prevailed: I am in derision daily, every one mocketh me. 8 For since I spake, I cried out, I cried violence and spoil; because the word of the LORD was made a reproach unto me, and a derision, daily. 9 Then I said, I will not make mention of him, nor speak any more in his name. But his word was in mine heart as a burning fire shut up in my bones, and I was weary with forbearing, and I could not stay. 10 For I heard the defaming of many, fear on every side. Report, say they, and we will report it. All my familiars watched for my halting, saying, Peradventure he will be enticed, and we shall prevail against him, and we shall take our revenge on him. 11 But the LORD is with me as a mighty terrible one: therefore my persecutors shall stumble, and they shall not prevail: they shall be greatly ashamed; for they shall not prosper: their everlasting confusion shall never be forgotten" Jer 20:7-11.

Jonah, Did Not Preach The Word Of God To Save Souls, Nor Did He Preach To Make Money For His Living, He Preached Out Of Envy And He Was Not Sincere.

The Bible said, "5 So Jonah went out of the city, and sat on the east side of the city, and there made him a booth, and sat under it in the shadow, till he might see what would become of the city. 6 And the LORD God prepared a gourd, and made it to come up over Jonah, that it might be a shadow over his head, to deliver him from his grief. So Jonah was exceeding glad of the gourd. 7 But God prepared a worm when the morning rose the next day, and it smote the gourd that it withered. 8 And it came to pass, when the sun did arise, that God prepared a vehement east wind; and the sun beat upon the head of Jonah, that he fainted, and wished in himself to die, and said, It is better for me to die than to live. 9 And God said to Jonah, Doest thou well to be angry for the gourd? And he said, I do well to be angry, even unto death. 10 Then said the LORD, Thou hast had pity on the gourd, for the which thou hast not laboured, neither madest it grow; which came up in a night, and perished in a night: 11 And should not I spare Nineveh, that great city, wherein are more than sixscore thousand persons that cannot discern between their right hand and their left hand; and also much cattle?" Jonah 4:5-11

Paul Explained To The Church In Philippi, That There Are Five Different Types Of Preachers, He Told Them That Some Preach Christ Out Of Envy, Some Of Strife, Some Of Good Will, Some Of Contention Not Sincerely, And Some Out Of Love.

Paul said, "15 And many of the brethren in the Lord, waxing confident by my bonds, are much more bold to speak the word without fear.15 Some indeed preach Christ even of envy and strife; and some also of good will: 16 The one preach Christ of contention, not sincerely, supposing to add affliction to my bonds: 17 But the other of love, knowing that I am set for the defence of the gospel. 18 What then? notwithstanding, every way, whether in pretence, or in truth, Christ is preached; and I therein do rejoice, yea, and will rejoice" Phil 1:15-18.

There Are Some Preachers Who Preach Completely Or Totally For Money To Make A Living For Themselves, To Those Preachers, Saving Souls Is Secondary; And Those Preachers May Not Be Aware That They Love Money.

Paul said, "10 For the love of money is the root of all evil: which while some coveted after, they have erred from the faith, and pierced themselves through with many sorrows. 11 But thou, O man of God, flee these things; and follow after righteousness, godliness, faith, love, patience, meekness. 12 Fight the good fight of faith, lay hold on eternal life, whereunto thou art also called, and hast professed a good profession before many witnesses" 1 Tim 6:10-12.

Paul Explained To The Church In Corinth, Concerning The Attitude Of Sincere Gospel Preachers.

Paul said, "5 For we preach not ourselves, but Christ Jesus the Lord; and ourselves your servants for Jesus' sake. 6 For God, who commanded the light to shine out of darkness, hath shined in our hearts, to give the light of the knowledge of the glory of God in the face of Jesus Christ. 7 But we have this treasure in earthen vessels, that the excellency of the power may be of God, and not of us. 8 We are troubled on every side, yet not distressed; we are perplexed, but not in despair; 9 Persecuted, but not forsaken; cast down, but not destroyed; 10 Always bearing about in the body the dying of the Lord Jesus, that the life also of Jesus might be made manifest in our body" 2 Cor 4:5-10.

Gospel Preachers, Who Are Preaching Sincerely, They Realize That They Are Commanded To Watch For People Souls.

Jeremiah said, "17 Also I set watchmen over you, *saying*, Hearken to the sound of the trumpet. But they said, We will not hearken" Jer 6:17.

The Hebrew writer said, "17 Obey them that have the rule over you, and submit yourselves: for they watch for your souls, as they that must give account, that they may do it with joy, and not with grief: for that *is* unprofitable for you: Heb 13:17.

Preachers, Who Are Preaching Completely Or Totally To Make Money For Themselves, Will Move From One Congregation To Another Only To Receive A Greater Pay.

Brethrens, The Churches Of Christ Need More Gospel Preacher As The Apostle Paul Was, Paul Preached The Gospel Of Christ In Some Places Freely.

Paul said, "7 Have I committed an offence in abasing myself that ye might be exalted, because I have preached to you the gospel of God freely? 8 I robbed other churches, taking wages of them, to do you service. 9 And when I was present with you, and wanted, I was chargeable to no man: for that which was lacking to me the brethren which came from Macedonia supplied: and in all things I have kept myself from being burdensome unto you, and so will I keep myself. 10 As the truth of Christ is in me, no man shall stop me of this boasting in the regions of Achaia" 2 Cor 11:7-10.

Paul Told Timothy, That If A Man Wanted To Be A Bishop, Tell Him That He Must Not Want That Office For To Make Money For Himself.

Paul said, "1 This is a true saying, If a man desire the office of a bishop, he desireth a good work. 2 A bishop then must be blameless, the husband of one wife, vigilant, sober, of good behaviour, given to hospitality, apt to teach; 3 Not given to wine, no striker, not greedy of filthy lucre; but patient, not a brawler, not covetous; 8 Likewise must the deacons be grave, not doubletongued, not given to much wine, not greedy of filthy lucre; 9 Holding the mystery of the faith in a pure conscience" 1 Tim 3:1-3, 8-9.

Jude, Made It Clear, That Preaching Is Not About Making Money For Oneself; Rather It Is For The Saving Of People Souls; Pulling Them Out Of The Fire Of Damnation.

Jude said, "20 But ye, beloved, building up yourselves on your most holy faith, praying in the Holy Ghost, 21 Keep yourselves in the love of God, looking for the mercy of our Lord Jesus Christ unto eternal life. 22 And of some have compassion, making a difference: 23 And others save with fear, pulling them out of the fire; hating even the garment spotted by the flesh. 24 Now unto him that is able to keep you from falling, and to present you faultless before the presence of his glory with exceeding joy, 25 To the only wise God our Saviour, be glory and majesty, dominion and power, both now and ever. Amen" Jude 1:20-25.

Gospel Preachers, Should Deny Themselves, And Follow Christ, Like He Told His Disciples To Do.

The Bible said, "24 Then said Jesus unto his disciples, If any man will come after me, let him deny himself, and take up his cross, and follow me. 25 For whosoever will save his life shall lose it: and whosoever will lose his life for my sake shall find it" Matt 16:24-25.

Gospel Preachers, Should Preach The Gospel As Christ Commanded Them To Do; Because He Is Our Example.

The Bible said, "9 Now when Jesus was risen early the first day of the week, he appeared first to Mary Magdalene, out of whom he had cast seven devils. 14 Afterward he appeared unto the eleven as they sat at meat, and upbraided them with their unbelief and hardness of heart, because they believed not them which had seen him after he was risen. 15 And he said unto them, Go ye into all the world, and preach the gospel to every creature. 16 He that believeth and is baptized shall be saved; but he that believeth not shall be damned" Mark 16:9, 14-16.

Peter said, "21 For even hereunto were ye called: because Christ also suffered for us, leaving us an example, that ye should follow his steps: 22 Who did no sin, neither was guile found in his mouth: 23 Who, when he was reviled, reviled not again; when he suffered, he threatened not; but committed himself to him that judgeth righteously: 24 Who his own self bare our sins in his own body on the tree, that we, being dead to sins, should live unto righteousness: by whose stripes ye were healed. 25 For ye were as sheep going astray; but are now returned unto the Shepherd and Bishop of your souls" 1 Peter 2:21-25.

Paul Told Titus, To Tell The Elders Of The Church, That He Ordained, That They Should Not Preach The Word Of God; To Make Money For Themselves

Paul said, "7 For a bishop must be blameless, as the steward of God; not selfwilled, not soon angry, not given to wine, no striker, not given to filthy lucre; 8 But a lover of hospitality, a lover of good men, sober, just, holy, temperate; 9 Holding fast the faithful word as he hath been taught, that he may be able by sound doctrine both to exhort and to convince the gainsayers" Titus 1:7-9.

Peter Told The Elders Of The Church, That He Ordained, That They Should Not Preach The Word Of God, To Make Money For Themselves

Peter said, "2 Feed the flock of God which is among you, taking the oversight thereof, not by constraint, but willingly; not for filthy lucre, but of a ready mind; 3 Neither as being lords over God's heritage, but being ensamples to the flock. 4 And when the chief Shepherd shall appear, ye shall receive a crown of glory that fadeth not away" 1 Peter 5:2-4.

All Gospel Preachers, Should Preach The Gospel Of Christ, Simply Because People Souls Are At State.

The Bible said, "16 Having a good conscience; that, whereas they speak evil of you, as of evildoers, they may be ashamed that falsely accuse your good conversation in Christ. 17 For it is better, if the will of God be so, that ye suffer for well doing, than for evil doing. 18 For Christ also hath once suffered for sins, the just for the unjust, that he might bring us to God, being put to death in the flesh, but quickened by the Spirit: 19 By which also he went and preached unto the spirits in prison; 20 Which sometime were disobedient, when once the longsuffering of God waited in the days of Noah, while the ark was a preparing, wherein few, that is, eight souls were saved by water. 21 The like figure whereunto even baptism doth also now save us (not the putting away of the filth of the flesh, but the answer of a good conscience toward God,) by the resurrection of Jesus Christ: 22 Who is gone into heaven, and is on the right hand of God; angels and authorities and powers being made subject unto him" 1 Peter 3:16-22.

All Gospel Preachers, Are Commanded By God, To Make Full Proof Of His Word.

Paul said, "21 Prove all things; hold fast that which is good'1 Thess 5:21.

Paul said, "1 I charge thee therefore before God, and the Lord Jesus Christ, who shall judge the quick and the dead at his appearing and his kingdom; 2 Preach the word; be instant in season, out of season; reprove, rebuke, exhort with all longsuffering and doctrine. 3 For the time will come when they will not endure sound doctrine; but after their own lusts shall they heap to themselves teachers, having itching ears; 4 And they shall turn away their ears from the truth, and shall be turned unto fables. 5 But watch thou in all things, endure afflictions, do the work of an evangelist, make full proof of thy ministry" 2 Tim 4:1-5.

The Trinity

In The Carnal World; The Word Trinity Means That There Are Three Divine Persons In The One God: The Father, The Son, And The Holy Spirit.

There Are Many Denominations, That Teach That The Trinity; Are Three Different Divine Beings In One Body: The Father, The Son, And The Holy Ghost; Now If That Doctrine Was True; That Would Mean That The God Of Heaven Is A Monster, With One Body, Six Arms, Six Legs, And Three Heads; That False Doctrine Is Of The Devil.

To Truly Understand The Family Of God, And The Godhead; We Need To Search The Scripture And Find Out What Does The Scripture Say, Concerning The Family Of God, And The Godhead: Let Us Start At The Beginning.

The Scripture Said, That In The Beginning God Created The Heaven And The Earth; So Then In The Beginning The Father God, Was In Heaven; The Son Of God, Which Was The Word, Was In Heaven, The Holy Ghost, Was In Heaven.

The Bible said, "1 In the beginning God created the heaven and the earth" Gen 1:1.

John said, "1 In the beginning was the Word, and the Word was with God, and the Word was God. 2 The same was in the beginning with

God. 14 And the Word was made flesh, and dwelt among us, (and we beheld his glory, the glory as of the only begotten of the Father,) full of grace and truth" John 1:1-2, 14.

John said, "7 For there are three that bear record in heaven, the Father, the Word, and the Holy Ghost: and these three are one" 1 John 5:7.

In The Family Of God; There Is Three Different Divine Beings Working In Unison With One Another In The Earth, To Save Mankind: The Spirit, The Water, And The Blood.

John said, "8 And there are three that bear witness in earth, the **Spirit**, and the **water**, and the **blood**: and these three **agree** in **one**" 1 John 5:8.

Paul said, "17 And take the helmet of salvation, and the **sword** of the **Spirit**, which is **the word of God**" Eph 6:17.

In Order For Mankind To Be Saved; They Must Hear The Word Of The SPIRIT, They Must Be BAPTIZED In The WATER, They Must Be REDEEM Through The BLOOD OF JESUS CHRIST, In This, These Three Agree In One.

John said, "17 And the **Spirit** and the **bride** say, **Come**. And let him that heareth say, Come. And let him that is athirst come. And whosoever will, let him take the water of life freely" Rev 22:17.

Paul said, "3 Know ye not, that so many of us as were baptized into Jesus Christ were baptized into his death? 4 Therefore we are buried with him by baptism into death: that like as Christ was raised up from the dead by the glory of the Father, even so we also should walk in newness of life" Romans 6:3-4.

Paul said, "7 In whom we have redemption through his blood, the forgiveness of sins, according to the riches of his grace" Eph 1:7.

Peter said, "18 Forasmuch as ye know that ye were not redeemed with corruptible things, as silver and gold, from your vain conversation received by tradition from your fathers; 19 But with the precious blood of Christ, as of a lamb without blemish and without spot" 1 Peter 1:18-19.

Paul Warned The Church Of Christ, Concerning Those That Are Teaching False Doctrines Of The Devil.

Paul said, "6 I marvel that ye are so soon removed from him that called you into the grace of Christ unto another gospel: 7 Which is not another; but there be some that trouble you, and would pervert the gospel of Christ. 8 But though we, or an angel from heaven, preach any other gospel unto you than that which we have preached unto you, let him be accursed. 9 As we said before, so say I now again, If any man preach any other gospel unto you than that ye have received, let him be accursed. 10 For do I now persuade men, or God? or do I seek to please men? for if I yet pleased men, I should not be the servant of Christ" Gal 1:6-10.

Paul Taught The Churches Of Christ, What The Godhead Is; And What It Is Not.

Paul said, "29 Forasmuch then as we are the offspring of God, we ought not to think that the Godhead is like unto gold, or silver, or stone, graven by art and man's device" Acts 17:29.

Paul said, "20 For the invisible things of him from the creation of the world are clearly seen, being understood by the things that are made, even his eternal power and Godhead; so that they are without excuse: 21 Because that, when they knew God, they glorified him not as God, neither were thankful; but became vain in their imaginations, and their foolish heart was darkened" Romans 1:20-21.

The Bible Teaches Some Infallible Proof; That God The Father And His Son Jesus Christ Are Not The Same One Divine Bodily Being.

Paul said, "8 Beware lest any man spoil you through philosophy and vain deceit, after the tradition of men, after the rudiments of the world, and not after Christ. 9 For in him dwelleth all the fulness of the Godhead bodily" Col 2:8-9.

Do You Believe That God The Father, Was Born In The City Of David; Or Do You Believe That His Son Jesus Christ Was?

The Bible said, "11 For unto you is born this day in the city of David a Saviour, which is Christ the Lord" Luke 2:11.

Do You Believe That After Christ Was Baptized, That The Voice Of God That He Heard From Heaven, Was His Own Voice?

The Bible said, "16 And Jesus, when he was baptized, went up straightway out of the water: and, lo, the heavens were opened unto him, and he saw the Spirit of God descending like a dove, and lighting upon him: 17 And lo a voice from heaven, saying, This is my beloved Son, in whom I am well pleased" Matt 3:16-17.

When Christ Was Dying On The Cross; He Cried Out To His Father, My God, My God, Why Hast Thou Forsaken Me; At That Time Do You Believe, That Christ Was crying Out To Himself?

The Bible said, "46 And about the ninth hour Jesus cried with a loud voice, saying, Eli, Eli, lama sabachthani? that is to say, My God, my God, why hast thou forsaken me?" Matt 27:46.

Do You Believe That After Christ Was Buried, That God The Father Raised Up His Son Jesus Christ From The Grave; Or Do You Believe That Jesus Christ Raised Himself Up From The Grave?

Paul said, "9 That if thou shalt confess with thy mouth the Lord Jesus, and shalt believe in thine heart that God hath raised him from the dead, thou shalt be saved" Romans 10:9.

Paul said, "14 Knowing that he which raised up the Lord Jesus shall raise up us also by Jesus, and shall present *us* with you" 2 Cor 4:14.

Paul said, "1 Paul, an apostle, (not of men, neither by man, but by Jesus Christ, and God the Father, who raised him from the dead" Gal 1:1.

If Mankind Would Understand That The God Of Heaven Is A Spirit; And That He Has Never Had Flesh And Bones: And That His Son Jesus Christ Had Flesh, And Bones; Then The Entire World Would Know, That God The Father, Jesus Christ His Son, Have Never Been One In The Bodily Form.

John said, "24 God *is* a Spirit: and they that worship him must worship *him* in spirit and in truth" John 4:24.

Jesus said, "39 Behold my hands and my feet, that it is I myself: handle me, and see; for a spirit hath not flesh and bones, as ye see me have" Luke 24:39.

The Bible said, "8 Philip saith unto him, Lord, shew us the Father, and it sufficeth us. 9 Jesus saith unto him, Have I been so long time with you, and yet hast thou not known me, Philip? he that hath seen me hath seen the Father; and how sayest thou then, Shew us the Father? 10 Believest thou not that I am in the Father, and the Father in me? the words that I speak unto you I speak not of myself: but the Father that dwelleth in me, he doeth the works. 11 Believe me that I am in the Father, and the Father in me: or else believe me for the very works' sake" John 14:8-11.

The Hebrew writer said, "1 God, who at sundry times and in divers manners spake in time past unto the fathers by the prophets, 2 Hath in these last days spoken unto us by his Son, whom he hath appointed heir of all things, by whom also he made the worlds; 3 Who being the brightness of his glory, and the express image of his person, and upholding all things by the word of his power, when he had by himself purged our sins, sat down on the right hand of the Majesty on high" Heb 1:1-3.

Jesus said, "17 Sanctify them through thy truth: thy word is truth. 18 As thou hast sent me into the world, even so have I also sent them into the world. 19 And for their sakes I sanctify myself, that they also might be sanctified through the truth" John 17:17-19.

Paul said, "20 Neither pray I for these alone, but for them also which shall believe on me through their word; 21 That they all may be one; as thou, Father, art in me, and I in thee, that they also may be one in us: that the world may believe that thou hast sent me. 22 And the glory which thou gavest me I have given them; that they may be one, even as we are one: 23 I in them, and thou in me, that they may be made perfect in one; and that the world may know that thou hast sent me, and hast loved them, as thou hast loved me" John 17:20-23.

Paul said, "24 Father, I will that they also, whom thou hast given me, be with me where I am; that they may behold my glory, which thou hast given me: for thou lovedst me before the foundation of the world. 25 O righteous Father, the world hath not known thee: but I have known thee, and these have known that thou hast sent me" John 17:24-25.

The Godhead Is A Family Of Three, And Like Most Families, They Are Call By The Father's Name: And The Family Name In Heaven Is God, And His Son Is Call God.

Paul said, "14 For this cause I bow my knees unto the Father of our Lord Jesus Christ, 15 Of whom the whole family in heaven and earth is named" Eph 3:14-15.

The Bible Said In Hebrew; That God The Father Call His Son God, Because That Is The Family Name.

The Hebrew writer said, "8 But unto the Son he saith, Thy throne, O God, is for ever and ever: a sceptre of righteousness is the sceptre of thy kingdom. 9 Thou hast loved righteousness, and hated iniquity; therefore God, even thy God, hath anointed thee with the oil of gladness above thy fellows" Heb 1:8-9.

If All Mankind Would Understand That We All Should Obey The Authority Of Jesus Christ, The Head Of The Church, The Same

As Jesus Christ, The Holy Ghost, And All Of The Heavenly Host Obey The Authority Of God The Father, The Head Of All Thing In Heaven: Then We All Would Speak The Same Thing Concerning The Churches Of Christ.

Paul said, "23 For the husband is the head of the wife, even as Christ is the head of the church: and he is the saviour of the body. 24 Therefore as the church is subject unto Christ, so let the wives be to their own husbands in every thing. 25 Husbands, love your wives, even as Christ also loved the church, and gave himself for it; 26 That he might sanctify and cleanse it with the washing of water by the word, 27 That he might present it to himself a glorious church, not having spot, or wrinkle, or any such thing; but that it should be holy and without blemish. 28 So ought men to love their wives as their own bodies. He that loveth his wife loveth himself. 29 For no man ever yet hated his own flesh; but nourisheth and cherisheth it, even as the Lord the church: 30 For we are members of his body, of his flesh, and of his bones. 31 For this cause shall a man leave his father and mother, and shall be joined unto his wife, and they two shall be one flesh. 32 This is a great mystery: but I speak concerning Christ and the church" Eph 5:23-32.

Jesus said, "18 And I say also unto thee, That thou art Peter, and upon this rock I will build my church; and the gates of hell shall not prevail against it" Matt 16:18.

Paul said, "16 Salute one another with an holy kiss. The churches of Christ salute you" Romans 16:16.

Paul said, "10 Now I beseech you, brethren, by the name of our Lord Jesus Christ, that ye all speak the same thing, and *that* there be no divisions among you; but *that* ye be perfectly joined together in the same mind and in the same judgment" 1 Cor 1:10.

The True Vine: The Husbandman: And The Branches

In The Beginning The Whole World Was One Nation, And One Language, And God Separated Them One From Another At The Tower Of Babel, To Live In All Parts Of The World, And Through The Process Of Time He Brought Those Nations Back Together On The Day Of Pentecost, In Jerusalem, At That Time He Made Them All One Nation, In Jesus Christ; And When The People Was Baptized Into Christ They Were Call Christians, And Christ Referred To Them As Branches.

Christ Said, "That He Was The True Vine.

Christ Said, "That His Father Was The Husbandman, Which Means That God Is The Keeper Of The Vine.

Christ Said, "That The Branches Are Those Who Have Been Baptized Into His Church.

Christ said, "1 I am the true vine, and my Father is the husbandman. 2 Every branch in me that beareth not fruit he taketh away: and every branch that beareth fruit, he purgeth it, that it may bring forth more fruit. 3 Now ye are clean through the word which I have spoken unto you. 4 Abide in me, and I in you. As the branch cannot bear fruit of itself, except it abide in the vine; no more can ye, except ye abide in me" John 15:1-4.

At The Last Passover, That Jesus Spent With His Disciple, He Took Bread And The Fruit Of The Vine, And He Instituted What Is Called The Lord's Supper, Or Communion.

The Bible said, "26 And as they were eating, Jesus took bread, and blessed it, and brake it, and gave it to the disciples, and said, Take, eat; this is my body. 27 And he took the cup, and gave thanks, and gave it to them, saying, Drink ye all of it; 28 For this is my blood of the new testament, which is shed for many for the remission of sins. 29 But I say unto you, I will not drink henceforth of this fruit of the vine, until that day when I drink it new with you in my Father's kingdom" Matt 26:26-29.

After Christ Was Raised From The Dead, He Commanded The Apostles To Go And Teach All Nations.

Jesus said, "19 Go ye therefore, and teach all nations, baptizing them in the name of the Father, and of the Son, and of the Holy Ghost: 20 Teaching them to observe all things whatsoever I have commanded you: and, lo, I am with you alway, even unto the end of the world. Amen" Matt 28:19-20.

The Bible said, "15 And he said unto them, Go ye into all the world, and preach the gospel to every creature. 16 He that believeth and is baptized shall be saved; but he that believeth not shall be damned" Mark 16:15-16.

On The Day Of Pentecost God Had Brought Every Nation, Under Heaven, To Jerusalem To Hear The Gospel Of Christ, Giving Them The Opportunity To Be Saved From Their Sins, And To Be Added To The Lord's Church.

The Bible said, "1 And when the day of Pentecost was fully come, they were all with one accord in one place. 5 And there were dwelling at Jerusalem Jews, devout men, out of every nation under heaven. 6 Now when this was noised abroad, the multitude came together, and were confounded, because that every man heard them speak in his own language. 7 And they were all amazed and marvelled, saying one to another, Behold, are not all these which speak Galilaeans? 8 And how hear we every man in our own tongue, wherein we were born? 9 Parthians, and Medes, and Elamites, and the dwellers in Mesopotamia, and in Judaea, and Cappadocia, in Pontus, and Asia, 10 Phrygia, and Pamphylia, in Egypt, and in the parts of Libya about Cyrene, and strangers of Rome, Jews and proselytes, 11 Cretes and Arabians, we do hear them speak in our tongues the wonderful works of God" Acts 2:1, 5-11.

The Bible said, "40 And with many other words did he testify and exhort, saying, Save yourselves from this untoward generation. 41 Then they that gladly received his word were baptized: and the same day there were added unto them about three thousand souls. 42 And they continued stedfastly in the apostles' doctrine and fellowship, and in breaking of bread, and in prayers. 43 And fear came upon every soul: and many wonders and signs were done by the apostles. 44 And all that believed were together, and had all things common" Acts 2:40-44.

Christ Came To Seek And To Save, That Which Was Lost.

The Bible said, "10 For the Son of man is come to seek and to save that which was lost" Luke 19:10.

Christ said, "16 And other sheep I have, which are not of this fold: them also I must bring, and they shall hear my voice; and there shall be one fold, and one shepherd. 17 Therefore doth my Father love me, because I lay down my life, that I might take it again. 18 No man taketh it from me, but I lay it down of myself. I have power to lay it down, and I have power to take it again. This commandment have I received of my Father" John 10:16-18.

Paul Explained That The Other Sheep That Christ Talked About Was The Gentiles Nation.

The Bible said, "45 But when the Jews saw the multitudes, they were filled with envy, and spake against those things which were spoken by Paul, contradicting and blaspheming. 46 Then Paul and Barnabas waxed bold, and said, It was necessary that the word of God should first have been spoken to you: but seeing ye put it from you, and judge yourselves unworthy of everlasting life, lo, we turn to the Gentiles. 47 For so hath the Lord commanded us, saying, I have set thee to be a light of the Gentiles, that thou shouldest be for salvation unto the ends of the earth. 48 And when the Gentiles heard this, they were glad, and glorified the word of the Lord: and as many as were ordained to eternal life believed" Acts 13:45-48.

Paul Explained The Gentiles Nation As The Wild Olive Tree That Was Grafted In.

Paul said, "13 For I speak to you Gentiles, inasmuch as I am the apostle of the Gentiles, I magnify mine office: 14 If by any means I may provoke to emulation them which are my flesh, and might save some of them. 15 For if the casting away of them be the reconciling of the world, what shall the receiving of them be, but life from the dead? 16 For if the firstfruit be holy, the lump is also holy: and if the root be holy, so are the branches. 17 And if some of the branches be broken off, and thou, being a wild olive tree, wert graffed in among them, and with them partakest of the root and fatness of the olive tree" Romans 11:13-17.

Paul said, "20 Well; because of unbelief they were broken off, and thou standest by faith. Be not highminded, but fear: 21 For if God spared not the natural branches, take heed lest he also spare not thee. 22 Behold therefore the goodness and severity of God: on them which fell, severity; but toward thee, goodness, if thou continue in his goodness: otherwise thou also shalt be cut off. 23 And they also, if they abide not still in unbelief, shall be graffed in: for God is able to graff them in again" Romans 11:20- 23.

Paul said, "11 Wherefore remember, that ye being in time past Gentiles in the flesh, who are called Uncircumcision by that which is called the Circumcision in the flesh made by hands; 12 That at that time ye were without Christ, being aliens from the commonwealth of Israel, and strangers from the covenants of promise, having no hope, and without God in the world: 13 But now in Christ Jesus ye who sometimes were far off are made nigh by the blood of Christ" Eph 2:11-13.

The Bible Talked About The Frame Of Mind That People Have, When They Hear The Word Of God.

The Bible said, "14 The sower soweth the word. 15 And these are they by the way side, where the word is sown (planted); but when they have heard, Satan cometh immediately, and taketh away the word that was sown in their hearts. 16 And these are they likewise which are sown (planted) on stony ground; who, when they have heard the word, immediately receive it with gladness; 17 And have no root in themselves, and so endure but for a time: afterward, when affliction or persecution ariseth for the word's sake, immediately they are offended. 18 And these are they which are sown (planted) among thorns; such as hear the word, 19 And the cares of this world, and the deceitfulness of riches, and the lusts of other things entering in, choke the word, and it becometh unfruitful. 20 And these are they which are sown (planted) on good ground; such as hear the word, and receive it, and bring forth fruit, some thirtyfold, some sixty, and some an hundred" Mark 4:14-20.

Peter, James, John, And Christ, Gave Warning To All Mankind, Concerning The Coming Of The Lord Jesus Christ.

Peter said, "9 The Lord is not slack concerning his promise, as some men count slackness; but is longsuffering to us-ward, not willing that any should perish, but that all should come to repentance. 10 But the day of the Lord will come as a thief in the night; in the which the heavens shall pass away with a great noise, and the elements shall melt with fervent heat, the earth also and the works that are therein shall be burned up. 11 Seeing then that all these things shall be dissolved, what manner of persons ought ye to be in all holy conversation and godliness, 12 Looking for and hasting unto the coming of the day of God, wherein the heavens being on fire shall be dissolved, and the elements shall melt with fervent heat?" 2 Peter 3:9-12.

James said, "7 Be patient therefore, brethren, unto the coming of the Lord. Behold, the husbandman waiteth for the precious fruit of the earth, and hath long patience for it, until he receive the early and latter rain. 8 Be ye also patient; stablish your hearts: for the coming of the Lord draweth nigh" James 5:7-8.

John said, "18 And another angel came out from the altar, which had power over fire; and cried with a loud cry to him that had the sharp sickle, saying, Thrust in thy sharp sickle, and gather the clusters of the vine of the earth; for her grapes are fully ripe. 19 And the angel thrust in his sickle into the earth, and gathered the vine of the earth, and cast it into the great winepress of the wrath of God" Rev 14:18-19.

Christ said, "5 I am the vine, ye are the branches: He that abideth in me, and I in him, the same bringeth forth much fruit: for without me ye can do nothing. 6 If a man abide not in me, he is cast forth as a branch, and is withered; and men gather them, and cast them into the fire, and they are burned. 7 If ye abide in me, and my words abide in you, ye shall ask what ye will, and it shall be done unto you. 8 Herein is my Father glorified, that ye bear much fruit; so shall ye be my disciples. 9 As the Father hath loved me, so have I loved you: continue ye in my love" John 15:5-9.

Time And Purpose

My Prayer To God Is That He Will Help Me To Explore Ecclesiastes 3:1-8. Thoroughly With You The Readers To Make Sure That We All Get The Full Understanding Of His Requirements, Concerning The Time, And The Purpose, That He Have Given Us.

According To The Scripture, Time And Purpose Is Something That God Give's To Every Living Thing Under The Heaven.

Solomon Said, "To Everything There Is A Season, And A Time To Every Purpose Under The Heaven".

Solomon said, "1 To every thing there is a season, and a time to every purpose under the heaven: 2 A time to be born, and a time to die; a time to plant, and a time to pluck up that which is planted; 3 A time to kill, and a time to heal; a time to break down, and a time to build up; 4 A time to weep, and a time to laugh; a time to mourn, and a time to dance; 5 A time to cast away stones, and a time to gather stones together; a time to embrace, and a time to refrain from embracing; 6 A time to get, and a time to lose; a time to keep, and a time to cast away; 7 A time to rend, and a time to sew; a time to keep silence, and a time to speak; 8 A time to love, and a time to hate; a time of war, and a time of peace" Eccl 3:1-8.

Solomon Said, "There Is A Time To Be Born".

Job said, "1 Man that is born of a woman is of few days, and full of trouble. 2 He cometh forth like a flower, and is cut down: he fleeth also as a shadow, and continueth not" Job 14:1-2.

David said, "3 Know ye that the LORD he *is* God: *it is* he *that* hath made us, and not we ourselves; *we are* his people, and the sheep of his pasture" Psalms 100:3.

The Bible said, "11 For unto you is born this day in the city of David a Saviour, which is Christ the Lord" Luke 2:11.

The Bible said, "3 Jesus answered and said unto him, Verily, verily, I say unto thee, Except a man be born again, he cannot see the kingdom of God. 4 Nicodemus saith unto him, How can a man be born when he is old? can he enter the second time into his mother's womb, and be born? 5 Jesus answered, Verily, verily, I say unto thee, Except a man be born of water and of the Spirit, he cannot enter into the kingdom of God. 6 That which is born of the flesh is flesh; and that which is born of the Spirit is spirit. 7 Marvel not that I said unto thee, Ye must be born again" John 3:3-7.

Solomon Said, "There Is A Time To Die".

Paul said, "6 For when we were yet without strength, in due time Christ died for the ungodly. 7 For scarcely for a righteous man will one die: yet peradventure for a good man some would even dare to die. 8 But God commendeth his love toward us, in that, while we were yet sinners, Christ died for us" Romans 5:6-8.

Solomon said, "10 Whatsoever thy hand findeth to do, do *it* with thy might; for *there is* no work, nor device, nor knowledge, nor wisdom, in the grave, whither thou goest" Eccl 9:10.

Solomon said, "1 Remember now thy Creator in the days of thy youth, while the evil days come not, nor the years draw nigh, when thou shalt say, I have no pleasure in them; 2 While the sun, or the light, or the moon, or the stars, be not darkened, nor the clouds return after the rain:

7 Then shall the dust return to the earth as it was: and the spirit shall return unto God who gave it" Eccl 12:1-2, 7.

Jesus said, "4 I must work the works of him that sent me, while it is day: the night cometh, when no man can work. 5 As long as I am in the world, I am the light of the world" John 9:4-5.

Paul said, "16 For the Lord himself shall descend from heaven with a shout, with the voice of the archangel, and with the trump of God: and the dead in Christ shall rise first: 17 Then we which are alive and remain shall be caught up together with them in the clouds, to meet the Lord in the air: and so shall we ever be with the Lord. 18 Wherefore comfort one another with these words" 1 Thess 4:16-18.

The Hebrew writer said, "27 And as it is appointed unto men once to die, but after this the judgment" Heb 9:27.

John said, "13 And I heard a voice from heaven saying unto me, Write, Blessed *are* the dead which die in the Lord from henceforth: Yea, saith the Spirit, that they may rest from their labours; and their works do follow them" Rev 14:13.

Solomon Said, "There Is A Time To Plant, And A Time To Pluck Up That Which Is Planted".

David said, "1 Except the LORD build the house, they labour in vain that build it: except the LORD keep the city, the watchman waketh *but* in vain" Psalms 127:1.

The Bible said, "12 Then came his disciples, and said unto him, Knowest thou that the Pharisees were offended, after they heard this saying? 13 But he answered and said, Every plant, which my heavenly Father hath not planted, shall be rooted up. 14 Let them alone: they be blind leaders of the blind. And if the blind lead the blind, both shall fall into the ditch" Matt 15:12-14.

Jesus said, "18 And I say also unto thee, That thou art Peter, and upon this rock I will build my church; and the gates of hell shall not prevail against it" Matt 16:18.

The Bible said, "14 The sower soweth the word. 15 And these are they by the way side, where the word is sown; but when they have heard, Satan cometh immediately, and taketh away the word that was sown in their hearts. 16 And these are they likewise which are sown on stony ground; who, when they have heard the word, immediately receive it with gladness; 17 And have no root in themselves, and so endure but for a time: afterward, when affliction or persecution ariseth for the word's sake, immediately they are offended. 18 And these are they which are sown among thorns; such as hear the word, 19 And the cares of this world, and the deceitfulness of riches, and the lusts of other things entering in, choke the word, and it becometh unfruitful. 20 And these are they which are sown on good ground; such as hear the word, and receive it, and bring forth fruit, some thirtyfold, some sixty, and some an hundred" Mark 4:14-20.

Paul said, "6 I have planted, Apollos watered; but God gave the increase. 7 So then neither is he that planteth any thing, neither he that watereth; but God that giveth the increase. 8 Now he that planteth and he that watereth are one: and every man shall receive his own reward according to his own labour. 9 For we are labourers together with God: ye are God's husbandry, ye are God's building" 1 Cor 3:6-9.

John said, "8 And unto the angel of the church in Smyrna write; These things saith the first and the last, which was dead, and is alive; 9 I know thy works, and tribulation, and poverty, (but thou art rich) and I know the blasphemy of them which say they are Jews, and are not, but are the synagogue of Satan" Rev 2:8-9.

Solomon Said, "There Is A Time To Kill".

Christ said, "28 And fear not them which kill the body, but are not able to kill the soul: but rather fear him which is able to destroy both soul and body in hell" Matt 10:28.

The Bible said, "31 And he began to teach them, that the Son of man must suffer many things, and be rejected of the elders, and *of* the chief priests, and scribes, and be killed, and after three days rise again" Mark 8:31.

The Bible said, "13 And there came a voice to him, Rise, Peter; kill, and eat. 14 But Peter said, Not so, Lord; for I have never eaten any thing that is common or unclean. 15 And the voice spake unto him again the second time, What God hath cleansed, that call not thou common" Acts 10:13-15.

Paul said, "14 For all the law is fulfilled in one word, even in this; Thou shalt love thy neighbour as thyself. 15 But if ye bite and devour one another, take heed that ye be not consumed one of another. 16 This I say then, Walk in the Spirit, and ye shall not fulfil the lust of the flesh" Gal 5:14-16.

Christ said, "10 The thief cometh not, but for to steal, and to kill, and to destroy: I am come that they might have life, and that they might have it more abundantly. 11 I am the good shepherd: the good shepherd giveth his life for the sheep" John 10:10-11.

Solomon Said, "There Is A Time To Heal".

The Bible said, "1 The Spirit of the Lord GOD is upon me; because the LORD hath anointed me to preach good tidings unto the meek; he hath sent me to bind up the brokenhearted, to proclaim liberty to the captives, and the opening of the prison to them that are bound; 2 To proclaim the acceptable year of the LORD, and the day of vengeance of our God; to comfort all that mourn" Isaiah 61:1-2.

Christ said, "6 But go rather to the lost sheep of the house of Israel. 7 And as ye go, preach, saying, The kingdom of heaven is at hand. 8 Heal the sick, cleanse the lepers, raise the dead, cast out devils: freely ye have received, freely give" Matt 10:6-8.

Christ said, "18 The Spirit of the Lord is upon me, because he hath anointed me to preach the gospel to the poor; he hath sent me to heal the brokenhearted, to preach deliverance to the captives, and recovering of sight to the blind, to set at liberty them that are bruised, 19 To preach the acceptable year of the Lord. 20 And he closed the book, and he gave it again to the minister, and sat down. And the eyes of all them that were in the synagogue were fastened on him" Luke 4:18-20.

James said, "14 Is any sick among you? let him call for the elders of the church; and let them pray over him, anointing him with oil in the name of the Lord: 15 And the prayer of faith shall save the sick, and the Lord shall raise him up; and if he have committed sins, they shall be forgiven him" James 5:14-15.

Solomon Said, "There Is A Time To Break Down, And A Time To Build Up".

Paul said, "14 For he is our peace, who hath made both one, and hath broken down the middle wall of partition between us; 15 Having abolished in his flesh the enmity, even the law of commandments contained in ordinances; for to make in himself of twain one new man, so making peace; 16 And that he might reconcile both unto God in one body by the cross, having slain the enmity thereby: 17 And came and preached peace to you which were afar off, and to them that were nigh" Eph 2:14-17.

Nehemiah said, "17 Then said I unto them, Ye see the distress that we are in, how Jerusalem lieth waste, and the gates thereof are burned with fire: come, and let us build up the wall of Jerusalem, that we be no more a reproach. 18 Then I told them of the hand of my God which was good upon me; as also the king's words that he had spoken unto me. And they said, Let us rise up and build. So they strengthened their hands for this good work" Neh 2:17-18.

Nehemiah said, "6 So built we the wall; and all the wall was joined together unto the half thereof: for the people had a mind to work" Neh 4:6.

Paul said, "7 But we have this treasure in earthen vessels, that the excellency of the power may be of God, and not of us. 8 We are troubled on every side, yet not distressed; we are perplexed, but not in despair; 9 Persecuted, but not forsaken; cast down, but not destroyed; 10 Always bearing about in the body the dying of the Lord Jesus, that the life also of Jesus might be made manifest in our body" 2 Cor 4:7-10.

Paul said, "1 We then, *as* workers together *with him*, beseech *you* also that ye receive not the grace of God in vain" 2 Cor 6:1.

Jude said, "20 But ye, beloved, building up yourselves on your most holy faith, praying in the Holy Ghost, 21 Keep yourselves in the love of God, looking for the mercy of our Lord Jesus Christ unto eternal life" Jude 1:20-21.

Solomon Said, "There Is A Time To Weep"

Paul said, "15 Rejoice with them that do rejoice, and weep with them that weep" Romans 12:15.

The Bible said, "75 And Peter remembered the word of Jesus, which said unto him, Before the cock crow, thou shalt deny me thrice. And he went out, and wept bitterly" Matt 26:75.

The Bible said, "28 But Jesus turning unto them said, Daughters of Jerusalem, weep not for me, but weep for yourselves, and for your children" Luke 23:28.

The Bible said, "34 And said, Where have ye laid him? They said unto him, Lord, come and see. 35 Jesus wept. 36 Then said the Jews, Behold how he loved him!" John 11:34-36

The Bible said, "1 In those days was Hezekiah sick unto death. And the prophet Isaiah the son of Amoz came to him, and said unto him, Thus saith the LORD, Set thine house in order; for thou shalt die, and not live. 2 Then he turned his face to the wall, and prayed unto the LORD, saying, 3 I beseech thee, O LORD, remember now how I have walked before thee in truth and with a perfect heart, and have done that which is good in thy sight. And Hezekiah wept sore" 2 Kings 20:1-3.

Solomon Said, "There Is A Time To Laugh"

Solomon said, "22 A merry heart doeth good *like* a medicine: but a broken spirit drieth the bones" Prov 17:22.

Christ said, "4 What man of you, having an hundred sheep, if he lose one of them, doth not leave the ninety and nine in the wilderness, and go after that which is lost, until he find it? 5 And when he hath found it, he layeth it on his shoulders, rejoicing. 6 And when he cometh home, he calleth together his friends and neighbours, saying unto them, Rejoice with me; for I have found my sheep which was lost. 7 I say unto you, that likewise joy shall be in heaven over one sinner that repenteth, more than over ninety and nine just persons, which need no repentance" Luke 15:4-7.

Christ said, "8 Either what woman having ten pieces of silver, if she lose one piece, doth not light a candle, and sweep the house, and seek diligently till she find it? 9 And when she hath found it, she calleth her friends and her neighbours together, saying, Rejoice with me; for I have found the piece which I had lost. 10 Likewise, I say unto you, there is joy in the presence of the angels of God over one sinner that repenteth" Luke 15:8-10.

David said, "1 Behold, how good and how pleasant it is for brethren to dwell together in unity! 2 It is like the precious ointment upon the head, that ran down upon the beard, even Aaron's beard: that went down to the skirts of his garments; 3 As the dew of Hermon, and as the dew that descended upon the mountains of Zion: for there the LORD commanded the blessing, even life for evermore" Psalms 133:1-3.

Solomon Said, "There Is A Time To Mourn"

Solomon said, "1 The Spirit of the Lord GOD is upon me; because the LORD hath anointed me to preach good tidings unto the meek; he hath sent me to bind up the brokenhearted, to proclaim liberty to the captives, and the opening of the prison to them that are bound; 2 To proclaim the acceptable year of the LORD, and the day of vengeance of our God; to comfort all that mourn; 3 To appoint unto them that mourn in Zion, to give unto them beauty for ashes, the oil of joy for mourning, the garment of praise for the spirit of heaviness; that they might be called trees of righteousness, the planting of the LORD, that he might be glorified" Isaiah 61:1-3.

Christ said, "4 Blessed *are* they that mourn: for they shall be comforted" Matt 5:4.

The Bible said, "1 And Sarah was an hundred and seven and twenty years old: these were the years of the life of Sarah. 2 And Sarah died in Kirjatharba; the same is Hebron in the land of Canaan: and Abraham came to mourn for Sarah, and to weep for her" Gen 23:1-2.

The Bible said, "32 Then when Mary was come where Jesus was, and saw him, she fell down at his feet, saying unto him, Lord, if thou hadst been here, my brother had not died. 33 When Jesus therefore saw her weeping, and the Jews also weeping which came with her, he groaned in the spirit, and was troubled" John 11:32-33.

Peter said, "6 Humble yourselves therefore under the mighty hand of God, that he may exalt you in due time: 7 Casting all your care upon him; for he careth for you" 1 Peter 5:6-7.

James said, "9 Be afflicted, and mourn, and weep: let your laughter be turned to mourning, and your joy to heaviness. 10 Humble yourselves in the sight of the Lord, and he shall lift you up" James 4:9-10.

Solomon Said, "There Is A Time To Dance"

The Bible said, "5 And David went out whithersoever Saul sent him, and behaved himself wisely: and Saul set him over the men of war, and he was accepted in the sight of all the people, and also in the sight of Saul's servants. 6 And it came to pass as they came, when David was returned from the slaughter of the Philistine, that the women came out of all cities of Israel, singing and dancing, to meet king Saul, with tabrets, with joy, and with instruments of musick. 7 And the women answered one another as they played, and said, Saul hath slain his thousands, and David his ten thousands" 1 Sam 18:5-7.

The Bible said, "11 For the LORD hath redeemed Jacob, and ransomed him from the hand of him that was stronger than he. 12 Therefore they shall come and sing in the height of Zion, and shall flow together to the goodness of the LORD, for wheat, and for wine, and for oil, and for the young of the flock and of the herd: and their soul shall be as a watered garden; and they shall not sorrow any more at all. 13 Then shall the virgin rejoice in the dance, both young men and old together: for I will turn their mourning into joy, and will comfort them, and make them rejoice from their sorrow. 14 And I will satiate the soul of the priests with fatness, and my people shall be satisfied with my goodness, saith the LORD" Jer 31:11-14.

The Bible said, "7 And he took him by the right hand, and lifted him up: and immediately his feet and ankle bones received strength. 8 And he leaping up stood, and walked, and entered with them into the temple, walking, and leaping, and praising God. 9 And all the people saw him walking and praising God" Acts 3:7-9.

Solomon Said, "There Is A Time, To Cast Away Stones"

Peter said, "8 And a stone of stumbling, and a rock of offence, *even to them* which stumble at the word, being disobedient: whereunto also they were appointed" 1 Peter 2:8.

The Bible said, "58 And cast him out of the city, and stoned him: and the witnesses laid down their clothes at a young man's feet, whose name was Saul. 59 And they stoned Stephen, calling upon God, and saying, Lord Jesus, receive my spirit. 60 And he kneeled down, and cried with a loud voice, Lord, lay not this sin to their charge. And when he had said this, he fell asleep" Acts 7:58-60.

Solomon Said, "There Is A Time To Gather Stones Together"

Christ said, "24 Therefore whosoever heareth these sayings of mine, and doeth them, I will liken him unto a wise man, which built his house upon a rock: 25 And the rain descended, and the floods came, and the winds blew, and beat upon that house; and it fell not: for it was founded upon a rock" Matt 7:24-25.

David said, "1 I waited patiently for the LORD; and he inclined unto me, and heard my cry. 2 He brought me up also out of an horrible pit, out of the miry clay, and set my feet upon a rock, and established my goings" Psalms 40:1-2.

Solomon Said, "There Is A Time To Embrace (Hold On To), And A Time To Refrain From Embracing (To Let Go Of)"

Solomon said, "7 Wisdom is the principal thing; therefore get wisdom: and with all thy getting get understanding. 8 Exalt her, and she shall promote thee: she shall bring thee to honour, when thou dost Embrace her. 9 She shall give to thine head an ornament of grace: a crown of glory shall she deliver to thee" Prov 4:7-9.

Solomon Said, "There Is A Time To Get"

Solomon said, "5 Get wisdom, get understanding: forget it not; neither decline from the words of my mouth. 6 Forsake her not, and she shall preserve thee: love her, and she shall keep thee" Prov 4:5-6.

Solomon Said, "There Is A Time To Lose"

Christ said, "39 He that findeth his life shall lose it: and he that loseth his life for my sake shall find it. 40 He that receiveth you receiveth me, and he that receiveth me receiveth him that sent me" Matt 10:39-40.

Peter said, "22 Seeing ye have purified your souls in obeying the truth through the Spirit unto unfeigned love of the brethren, see that ye love one another with a pure heart fervently: 23 Being born again, not of corruptible seed, but of incorruptible, by the word of God, which liveth and abideth for ever" 1 Peter 1:22-23.

Solomon Said, "There Is A Time To Keep"

Paul said, "9 In like manner also, that women adorn themselves in modest apparel, with shamefacedness and sobriety; not with broided hair, or gold, or pearls, or costly array; 10 But (which becometh women professing godliness) with good works. 11 Let the woman learn in silence with all subjection. 12 But I suffer not a woman to teach, nor to usurp authority over the man, but to be in silence" 1 Tim 2:9-12.

Paul said, "18 That they do good, that they be rich in good works, ready to distribute, willing to communicate; 19 Laying up in store for themselves a good foundation against the time to come, that they may lay hold on eternal life. 20 O Timothy, keep that which is committed to thy trust, avoiding profane and vain babblings, and oppositions of science falsely so called" 1 Tim 6:18-20:

Jude said, "21 Keep yourselves in the love of God, looking for the mercy of our Lord Jesus Christ unto eternal life" Jude 1:21.

Solomon Said, "There Is A Time To Cast Away"

Solomon said, "17 A proud look, a lying tongue, and hands that shed innocent blood, 18 An heart that deviseth **wicked imaginations**, feet that be swift in running to mischief, 19 A false witness that speaketh lies, and he that soweth discord among brethren" Prov 6:17-19.

Peter said, "7 Casting all your care upon him; for he careth for you" 1 Peter 5:7.

Solomon Said, "There Is A Time To Rend"

Christ said, "25 Woe unto you, scribes and Pharisees, hypocrites! for ye make clean the outside of the cup and of the platter, but within they are full of extortion and excess. 26 Thou blind Pharisee, cleanse first that which is within the cup and platter, that the outside of them may be clean also" Matt 23:25-26.

Paul said, "22 That ye put off concerning the former conversation the old man, which is corrupt according to the deceitful lusts; 23 And be renewed in the spirit of your mind; 24 And that ye put on the new man, which after God is created in righteousness and true holiness. 25 Wherefore putting away lying, speak every man truth with his neighbour: for we are members one of another" Eph 4:22-25.

Solomon Said, "There Is A Time To Sew"

Christ said, "16 No man putteth a piece of new cloth unto an old garment, for that which is put in to fill it up taketh from the garment, and the rent is made worse" Matt 9:16.

The Bible said, "17 Then said I unto them, Ye see the distress that we *are* in, how Jerusalem *lieth* waste, and the gates thereof are burned with fire: come, and let us build up the wall of Jerusalem, that we be no more a reproach" Neh 2:17.

Solomon Said, "There Is Time To Keep Silence"

The Bible said, "13 And Moses said unto the people, Fear ye not, stand still, and see the salvation of the LORD, which he will shew to you to day: for the Egyptians whom ye have seen to day, ye shall see them again no more for ever. 14 The LORD shall fight for you, and ye shall hold your peace" Ex 14:13-14.

Paul said, "12 But I suffer not a woman to teach, nor to usurp authority over the man, but to be in silence" 1 Tim 2:12.

Paul said, "27 If any man speak in an unknown tongue, let it be by two, or at the most by three, and that by course; and let one interpret. 28 But if there be no interpreter, let him keep silence in the church; and let him speak to himself, and to God. 29 Let the prophets speak two or three, and let the other judge" 1 Cor 14:27-29.

Solomon Said, "There Is A Time To Speak"

The Bible said, "1 Then Agrippa said unto Paul, Thou art permitted to speak for thyself. Then Paul stretched forth the hand, and answered for himself: 2 I think myself happy, king Agrippa, because I shall answer for myself this day before thee touching all the things whereof I am accused of the Jews: 3 Especially because I know thee to be expert in all customs and questions which are among the Jews: wherefore I beseech thee to hear me patiently" Acts 26:1-3.

James said, "19 Wherefore, my beloved brethren, let every man be swift to hear, slow to speak, slow to wrath: 20 For the wrath of man worketh not the righteousness of God" James 1:19-20.

Solomon Said, "There Is A Time To Love"

The Bible said, "16 For God so loved the world, that he gave his only begotten Son, that whosoever believeth in him should not perish, but have everlasting life" John 3:16.

The Bible said, "7 The LORD did not set his love upon you, nor choose you, because ye were more in number than any people; for ye were the fewest of all people: 8 But because the LORD loved you, and because he would keep the oath which he had sworn unto your fathers, hath the LORD brought you out with a mighty hand, and redeemed you out of the house of bondmen, from the hand of Pharaoh king of Egypt" Deut 7:7-8.

Solomon said, "17 I love them that love me; and those that seek me early shall find me" Prov 8:17.

Solomon said, "12 Hatred stirreth up strifes: but love covereth all sins" Prov 10:12.

Paul said, "8 Owe no man any thing, but to love one another: for he that loveth another hath fulfilled the law, 10 Love worketh no ill to his neighbour: therefore love *is* the fulfilling of the law" Romans 13:8, 10.

Paul said, "6 For in Jesus Christ neither circumcision availeth any thing, nor uncircumcision; but faith which worketh by love" Gal 5:6.

James said, "19 Brethren, if any of you do err from the truth, and one convert him; 20 Let him know, that he which converteth the sinner from the error of his way shall save a soul from death, and shall hide a multitude of sins" James 5:19-20.

Peter said, "22 Seeing ye have purified your souls in obeying the truth through the Spirit unto unfeigned love of the brethren, see that ye love one another with a pure heart fervently: 23 Being born again, not of corruptible seed, but of incorruptible, by the word of God, which liveth and abideth for ever" 1 Peter 1:22-23.

People Of The World; It Is Time For All Mankind To Let Go Of The Biases And Prejudices That Has Plagued Our World Far Too Long, And Embrace The Love That We Should Have For One Another.

Solomon Said, "There Is A Time To Hate"

The Bible said, "43 Ye have heard that it hath been said, Thou shalt love thy neighbour, and hate thine enemy. 44 But I say unto you, Love your enemies, bless them that curse you, do good to them that hate you, and pray for them which despitefully use you, and persecute you; 45 That ye may be the children of your Father which is in heaven: for he maketh his sun to rise on the evil and on the good, and sendeth rain on the just and on the unjust" Matt 5:43-45.

The Bible said, "9 Know therefore that the LORD thy God, he is God, the faithful God, which keepeth covenant and mercy with them that love him and keep his commandments to a thousand generations; 10 And repayeth them that hate him to their face, to destroy them: he will not be slack to him that hateth him, he will repay him to his face" Deut 7:9-10.

The Bible said, "17 Thou shalt not hate thy brother in thine heart: thou shalt in any wise rebuke thy neighbour, and not suffer sin upon him" Lev 19:17.

Christ said, "24 No man can serve two masters: for either he will hate the one, and love the other; or else he will hold to the one, and despise the other. Ye cannot serve God and mammon" Matt 6:24.

Solomon Said, "There Is A Time Of War"

Paul said, "10 Finally, my brethren, be strong in the Lord, and in the power of his might. 11 Put on the whole armour of God, that ye may be able to stand against the wiles of the devil. 12 For we wrestle not against flesh and blood, but against principalities, against powers, against the rulers of the darkness of this world, against spiritual wickedness in high places. 13 Wherefore take unto you the whole armour of God, that ye may be able to withstand in the evil day, and having done all, to stand" Eph 6:10-13.

Paul said, "18 This charge I commit unto thee, son Timothy, according to the prophecies which went before on thee, that thou by them mightest war a good warfare; 19 Holding faith, and a good conscience; which some having put away concerning faith have made shipwreck" 1 Tim 1:18-19.

Paul said, "12 Fight the good fight of faith, lay hold on eternal life, whereunto thou art also called, and hast professed a good profession before many witnesses" 1 Tim 6:12.

Paul said, "3 Thou therefore endure hardness, as a good soldier of Jesus Christ. 4 No man that warreth entangleth himself with the affairs of this life; that he may please him who hath chosen him to be a soldier" 2 Tim 2:3-4.

Paul said, "6 For I am now ready to be offered, and the time of my departure is at hand. 7 I have fought a good fight, I have finished my course, I have kept the faith: 8 Henceforth there is laid up for me a crown of righteousness, which the Lord, the righteous judge, shall give me at that day: and not to me only, but unto all them also that love his appearing" 2 Tim 4:6-8.

James said, "1 From whence come wars and fightings among you? come they not hence, even of your lusts that war in your members? 2 Ye lust, and have not: ye kill, and desire to have, and cannot obtain: ye fight and war, yet ye have not, because ye ask not" James 4:1-2.

Solomon Said, "There Is A Time Of Peace"

Christ said, "9 Blessed *are* the peacemakers: for they shall be called the children of God" Matt 5:9.

Paul said, "33 For God is not *the author* of confusion, but of peace, as in all churches of the saints" 1 Cor 14:33.

John said, "27 Peace I leave with you, my peace I give unto you: not as the world giveth, give I unto you. Let not your heart be troubled, neither let it be afraid" John 14:27.

Paul said, "17 Recompense to no man evil for evil. Provide things honest in the sight of all men. 18 If it be possible, as much as lieth in you, live peaceably with all men. 19 Dearly beloved, avenge not yourselves, but rather give place unto wrath: for it is written, Vengeance is mine; I will repay, saith the Lord. 20 Therefore if thine enemy hunger, feed him; if he thirst, give him drink: for in so doing thou shalt heap coals of fire on his head. 21 Be not overcome of evil, but overcome evil with good" Romans 12:17-21.

Paul said, "15 And let the peace of God rule in your hearts, to the which also ye are called in one body; and be ye thankful" Col 3:15.

Gazing Into Heaven

Gazing Into Heaven; Means To Fix Your Eyes, And Stay Focused As You Wait To See Jesus When He Come Again, And Be Ready To Go To Heaven With Him When He Come!

The Bible said, "8 But ye shall receive power, after that the Holy Ghost is come upon you: and ye shall be witnesses unto me both in Jerusalem, and in all Judaea, and in Samaria, and unto the uttermost part of the earth. 9 And when he had spoken these things, while they beheld, he was taken up; and a cloud received him out of their sight. 10 And while they looked stedfastly toward heaven as he went up, behold, two men stood by them in white apparel; 11 Which also said, Ye men of Galilee, why stand ye gazing up into heaven? this same Jesus, which is taken up from you into heaven, shall so come in like manner as ye have seen him go into heaven" Acts 1:8-11.

Staying Focused On Going To Heaven, Means That You Have To Be Watchful, And You Have To Stay Instant In Prayer.

Christ said, "13 Watch therefore, for ye know neither the day nor the hour wherein the Son of man cometh" Matt 25:13.

Christ said, "41 Watch and pray, that ye enter not into temptation: the spirit indeed *is* willing, but the flesh *is* weak" Matt 26:41.

Christ said, "36 Watch ye therefore, and pray always, that ye may be accounted worthy to escape all these things that shall come to pass, and to stand before the Son of man" Luke 21:36.

Paul said, "13 Watch ye, stand fast in the faith, quit you like men, be strong" 1 Cor 16:13.

Paul said, "12 Rejoicing in hope; patient in tribulation; continuing instant in prayer" Romans 12:12;

Paul said, "17 Pray without ceasing" 1 Thess 5:17.

Staying Focused On Going To Heaven, Means That You Have To Forget Your Pass.

Paul said, "17 Therefore if any man be in Christ, he is a new creature: old things are passed away; behold, all things are become new. 18 And all things are of God, who hath reconciled us to himself by Jesus Christ, and hath given to us the ministry of reconciliation; 19 To wit, that God was in Christ, reconciling the world unto himself, not imputing their trespasses unto them; and hath committed unto us the word of reconciliation" 2 Cor 5:17-19.

Paul said, "13 Brethren, I count not myself to have apprehended: but this one thing I do, forgetting those things which are behind, and reaching forth unto those things which are before" Phil 3:13.

Staying Focused On Going To Heaven, Means That Men Have To Fight The Good Fight Of Faith; And They Have To Stay Focused On The Reward That Is Waiting For Them In Heaven.

Paul said, "14 I press toward the mark for the prize of the high calling of God in Christ Jesus" Phil 3:14.

Paul said, "7 I have fought a good fight, I have finished my course, I have kept the faith: 8 Henceforth there is laid up for me a crown of righteousness, which the Lord, the righteous judge, shall give me at that day: and not to me only, but unto all them also that love his appearing" 2 Tim 4:7-8.

Staying Focused On Going To Heaven, Means That Sometime You Have To Pray For Your Enemies.

Christ said, "44 But I say unto you, Love your enemies, bless them that curse you, do good to them that hate you, and pray for them which despitefully use you, and persecute you; 45 That ye may be the children of your Father which is in heaven: for he maketh his sun to rise on the evil and on the good, and sendeth rain on the just and on the unjust" Matt 5:44-45.

Christ said, "12 And forgive us our debts, as we forgive our debtors. 13 And lead us not into temptation, but deliver us from evil: For thine is the kingdom, and the power, and the glory, for ever. Amen. 14 For if ye forgive men their trespasses, your heavenly Father will also forgive you: 15 But if ye forgive not men their trespasses, neither will your Father forgive your trespasses" Matt 6:12-15.

The Bible said, "34 Then said Jesus, Father, forgive them; for they know not what they do. And they parted his raiment, and cast lots" Luke 23:34.

The Bible said, "60 And he kneeled down, and cried with a loud voice, Lord, lay not this sin to their charge. And when he had said this, he fell asleep" Acts 7:60.

Let Us Gaze Into Heaven, Through The Eyes Of Stephen.

The Bible said, "54 When they heard these things, they were cut to the heart, and they gnashed on him with their teeth. 55 But he, being full of the Holy Ghost, looked up stedfastly into heaven, and saw the glory of God, and Jesus standing on the right hand of God, 56 And said, Behold, I see the heavens opened, and the Son of man standing on the right hand of God" Acts 7:54-56.

Let Us Gaze Into Heaven, Through The Eyes Of Paul.

Paul said, "1 It is not expedient for me doubtless to glory. I will come to visions and revelations of the Lord. 2 I knew a man in Christ above fourteen years ago, (whether in the body, I cannot tell; or whether out of the body, I cannot tell: God knoweth;) such an one caught up to the third heaven. 3 And I knew such a man, (whether in the body, or out of the body, I cannot tell: God knoweth;) 4 How that he was caught up into paradise, and heard unspeakable words, which it is not lawful for a man to utter" 2 Cor 12:1-4.

Let Us Gaze Into Heaven, Through The Eyes Of John.
John Said, He Saw The Book Of Life.

John said, "1 After this I looked, and, behold, a door was opened in heaven: and the first voice which I heard was as it were of a trumpet talking with me; which said, Come up hither, and I will shew thee things which must be hereafter" Rev 4:1.

John said, "1 And I saw in the right hand of him that sat on the throne a book written within and on the backside, sealed with seven seals" Rev 5:1.

John said, "8 The beast that thou sawest was, and is not; and shall ascend out of the bottomless pit, and go into perdition: and they that dwell on the earth shall wonder, whose names were not written in the book of life from the foundation of the world, when they behold the beast that was, and is not, and yet is" Rev 17:8.

John Said, He Saw The New Heaven, The New Earth, And The New Jerusalem, And He Describe The Beauty Of Them.

John said, "1 And I saw a new heaven and a new earth: for the first heaven and the first earth were passed away; and there was no more sea. 2 And I John saw the holy city, new Jerusalem, coming down from God out of heaven, prepared as a bride adorned for her husband. 3 And I heard a great voice out of heaven saying, Behold, the tabernacle of God is with men, and he will dwell with them, and they shall be his people, and God himself shall be with them, and be their God. 4 And God shall wipe away all tears from their eyes; and there shall be no more death, neither sorrow, nor crying, neither shall there be any more pain: for the former things are passed away. 5 And he that sat upon the throne said, Behold, I make all things new. And he said unto me, Write: for these words are true and faithful. 6 And he said unto me, It is done. I am Alpha and Omega, the beginning and the end. I will give unto him that is athirst of the fountain of the water of life freely" Rev 21:1-6.

John said, "23 And the city had no need of the sun, neither of the moon, to shine in it: for the glory of God did lighten it, and the Lamb is the light thereof. 24 And the nations of them which are saved shall walk in the light of it: and the kings of the earth do bring their glory and honour into it. 25 And the gates of it shall not be shut at all by day: for there shall be no night there. 26 And they shall bring the glory and honour of the nations into it. 27 And there shall in no wise enter into it any thing that defileth, neither whatsoever worketh abomination, or maketh a lie: but they which are written in the Lamb's book of life" Rev 21:23-27.

John Said, He Saw The Water Of Life, The Throne Of God, And Of The Lamb, And The Tree Of Life.

John said, "1 1 And he shewed me a pure river of water of life, clear as crystal, proceeding out of the throne of God and of the Lamb. And he shewed me a pure river of water of life, clear as crystal, proceeding out of the throne of God and of the Lamb. 2 In the midst of the street of it, and on either side of the river, was there the tree of life, which bare twelve manner of fruits, and yielded her fruit every month: and the leaves of the tree were for the healing of the nations. 3 And there shall be no more curse: but the throne of God and of the Lamb shall be in it; and his servants shall serve him: 4 And they shall see his face; and his name shall be in their foreheads" Rev 22:1-4.

John Said, He Saw The Building; And The Street Of The City, And He Describe The Beauty Of Them.

John said, "18 And the of the wall of it was of jasper: and the city was pure gold, like unto clear glass. 19 And the foundations of the wall of the city were garnished with all manner of precious stones. The first foundation was jasper; the second, sapphire; the third, a chalcedony; the fourth, an emerald; 20 The fifth, sardonyx; the sixth, sardius; the seventh, chrysolite; the eighth, beryl; the ninth, a topaz; the tenth, a chrysoprasus; the eleventh, a jacinth; the twelfth, an amethyst. 21 And the twelve gates were twelve pearls; every several gate was of one pearl: and the street of the city was pure gold, as it were transparent glass" Rev 21:18-21.

John Said, He Saw What Will Happen To The People In The End.

John said, "11 He that is unjust, let him be unjust still: and he which is filthy, let him be filthy still: and he that is righteous, let him be righteous still: and he that is holy, let him be holy still. 12 And, behold, I come quickly; and my reward is with me, to give every man according as his work shall be. 13 I am Alpha and Omega, the beginning and the end, the first and the last. 14 Blessed are they that do his commandments, that they may have right to the tree of life, and may enter in through the gates into the city. 15 For without are dogs, and sorcerers, and whoremongers, and murderers, and idolaters, and whosoever loveth and maketh a lie" Rev 22:11-15.

John said, "16 I Jesus have sent mine angel to testify unto you these things in the churches. I am the root and the offspring of David, and the bright and morning star. 17 And the Spirit and the bride say, Come. And let him that heareth say, Come. And let him that is athirst come. And whosoever will, let him take the water of life freely. 18 For I testify unto every man that heareth the words of the prophecy of this book, If any man shall add unto these things, God shall add unto him the plagues that are written in this book: 19 And if any man shall take away from the words of the book of this prophecy, God shall take away his part out of the book of life, and out of the holy city, and from the things which are written in this book. 20 He which testifieth these things saith, Surely I come quickly. Amen. Even so, come, Lord Jesus. 21 The grace of our Lord Jesus Christ be with you all. Amen" Rev 22:16-21.

John said, "14 And the heaven departed as a scroll when it is rolled together; and every mountain and island were moved out of their places. 15 And the kings of the earth, and the great men, and the rich men, and the chief captains, and the mighty men, and every bondman, and every free man, hid themselves in the dens and in the rocks of the mountains; 16 And said to the mountains and rocks, Fall on us, and hide us from the face of him that sitteth on the throne, and from the wrath of the Lamb: 17 For the great day of his wrath is come; and who shall be able to stand?" Rev 6:14-17

Paul said, "24 Then cometh the end, when he shall have delivered up the kingdom to God, even the Father; when he shall have put down all rule and all authority and power. 25 For he must reign, till he hath put all enemies under his feet. 26 The last enemy that shall be destroyed is death" 1 Cor 15:24-26.

Paul said, "16 For the Lord himself shall descend from heaven with a shout, with the voice of the archangel, and with the trump of God: and the dead in Christ shall rise first: 17 Then we which are alive and remain shall be caught up together with them in the clouds, to meet the Lord in the air: and so shall we ever be with the Lord. 18 Wherefore comfort one another with these words" 1 Thess 4:16-18.

Peter said, "17 For the time is come that judgment must begin at the house of God: and if it first begin at us, what shall the end be of them that obey not the gospel of God? 18 And if the righteous scarcely be saved, where shall the ungodly and the sinner appear? 19 Wherefore let them that suffer according to the will of God commit the keeping of their souls to him in well doing, as unto a faithful Creator" 1 Peter 4:17-19.

John said, "12 And I saw the dead, small and great, stand before God; and the books were opened: and another book was opened, which is the book of life: and the dead were judged out of those things which were written in the books, according to their works. 13 And the sea gave up the dead which were in it; and death and hell delivered up the dead which were in them: and they were judged every man according to their works. 14 And death and hell were cast into the lake of fire. This is the second death. 15 And whosoever was not found written in the book of life was cast into the lake of fire" Rev 20:12-15.

Hope

Hope; Mean To Expect Or Anticipate On Receiving Something That Is Not Seen.

The Bible Teaches That Sinners Are Saved By Hope.

Paul said, "1 Therefore being justified by faith, we have peace with God through our Lord Jesus Christ: 2 By whom also we have access by faith into this grace wherein we stand, and rejoice in hope of the glory of God. 3 And not only so, but we glory in tribulations also: knowing that tribulation worketh patience; 4 And patience, experience; and experience, hope: 5 And hope maketh not ashamed; because the love of God is shed abroad in our hearts by the Holy Ghost which is given unto us. 6 For when we were yet without strength, in due time Christ died for the ungodly" Romans 5:1-6.

Paul said, "16 For I am not ashamed of the gospel of Christ: for it is the power of God unto salvation to every one that believeth; to the Jew first, and also to the Greek. 17 For therein is the righteousness of God revealed from faith to faith: as it is written, The just shall live by faith"

Romans 1:16-17.

Paul said, "13 Therefore we were comforted in your comfort: yea, and exceedingly the more joyed we for the joy of Titus, because his spirit was refreshed by you all. 14 For if I have boasted any thing to him of you, I am not ashamed; but as we spake all things to you in truth, even so our boasting, which I made before Titus, is found a truth. 15 And his inward affection is more abundant toward you, whilst he remembereth the obedience of you all, how with fear and trembling ye received him. 16 I rejoice therefore that I have confidence in you in all things" 2 Cor 7:13-16.

Paul said, "20 According to my earnest expectation and my hope, that in nothing I shall be ashamed, but that with all boldness, as always, so now also Christ shall be magnified in my body, whether it be by life, or by death. 21 For to me to live is Christ, and to die is gain" Phil 1:20-21.

Paul said, "15 Now ye Philippians know also, that in the beginning of the gospel, when I departed from Macedonia, no church communicated with me as concerning giving and receiving, but ye only. 16 For even in Thessalonica ye sent once and again unto my necessity" Phil 4:15-16.

The Bible Teaches That Faith, And Hope, Bring About Things That Are Not Previously Seen.

The Hebrew writer said, "1 Now faith is the substance of things hoped for, the evidence of things not seen" Heb 11:1.

Paul said, "24 For we are saved by hope: but hope that is seen is not hope: for what a man seeth, why doth he yet hope for? 25 But if we hope for that we see not, then do we with patience wait for it. 26 Likewise the Spirit also helpeth our infirmities: for we know not what we should pray for as we ought: but the Spirit itself maketh intercession for us with groanings which cannot be uttered. 27 And he that searcheth the hearts knoweth what is the mind of the Spirit, because he maketh intercession for the saints according to the will of God" Romans 8:24-27.

The Bible Teaches, The People; Who's Hope Is Deferred Have Nothing To Look Forward To, But The Fiery Indignation Of Hell.

Solomon said, "12 Hope deferred maketh the heart sick: but when the desire cometh, it is a tree of life. 13 Whoso despiseth the word shall be destroyed: but he that feareth the commandment shall be rewarded" Prov 13:12-13.

The Hebrew writer said, "Heb 10:25-27 25 Not forsaking the assembling of ourselves together, as the manner of some is; but exhorting one another: and so much the more, as ye see the day approaching. 26 For if we sin wilfully after that we have received the knowledge of the truth, there remaineth no more sacrifice for sins, 27 But a certain fearful looking for of judgment and fiery indignation, which shall devour the adversaries.

The Bible Teaches That The Christians Who Have Hope; Must Stay Continually In Prayer.

Paul said, "12 Rejoicing in hope; patient in tribulation; continuing instant in prayer" Romans 12:12.

Paul said, "17 Pray without ceasing" 1 Thess 5:17.

Paul said, "18 Praying always with all prayer and supplication in the Spirit, and watching thereunto with all perseverance and supplication for all saints; 19 And for me, that utterance may be given unto me, that I may open my mouth boldly, to make known the mystery of the gospel, 20 For which I am an ambassador in bonds: that therein I may speak boldly, as I ought to speak" Eph 6:18-20.

It Is Very Crucial For Christians, And So-Called Christians, To Search The Scriptures Daily, To Make Sure That They Are Saved.

John said, "39 Search the scriptures; for in them ye think ye have eternal life: and they are they which testify of me" John 5:39.

Paul said, "4 For whatsoever things were written aforetime were written for our learning, that we through patience and comfort of the scriptures might have hope. 13 Now the God of hope fill you with all joy and peace in believing, that ye may abound in hope, through the power of the Holy Ghost. 14 And I myself also am persuaded of you, my brethren, that ye also are full of goodness, filled with all knowledge, able also to admonish one another" Romans 15:4, 13-14.

Paul said, "15 And that from a child thou hast known the holy scriptures, which are able to make thee wise unto salvation through faith which is in Christ Jesus. 16 All scripture is given by inspiration of God, and is profitable for doctrine, for reproof, for correction, for instruction in righteousness: 17 That the man of God may be perfect, throughly furnished unto all good works" 2 Tim 3:15-17.

Paul said, "11 These were more noble than those in Thessalonica, in that they received the word with all readiness of mind, and searched the scriptures daily, whether those things were so" Acts 17:11.

People, Who Are Not In The Church Of Christ, Have No Hope Of Salvation.

Paul said, "12 That at that time ye were without Christ, being aliens from the commonwealth of Israel, and strangers from the covenants of promise, having no hope, and without God in the world: 13 But now in Christ Jesus ye who sometimes were far off are made nigh by the blood of Christ" Eph 2:12-13.

Paul said, "10 Therefore I endure all things for the elect's sakes, that they may also obtain the salvation which is in Christ Jesus with eternal glory. 11 It is a faithful saying: For if we be dead with him, we shall also live with him: 12 If we suffer, we shall also reign with him: if we deny him, he also will deny us" 2 Tim 2:10-12.

Peter said, "10 Be it known unto you all, and to all the people of Israel, that by the name of Jesus Christ of Nazareth, whom ye crucified, whom God raised from the dead, even by him doth this man stand here before you whole. 11 This is the stone which was set at nought of you builders, which is become the head of the corner. 12 Neither is there salvation in any other: for there is none other name under heaven given among men, whereby we must be saved" Acts 4:10-12.

The Bible Teaches That The Reality Of Hope; Is Proven By The Things That People Have Gained, Or Have Accomplished Through Hope.

The Bible said, "33 And he shall set the sheep on his right hand, but the goats on the left. 34 Then shall the King say unto them on his right hand, Come, ye blessed of my Father, inherit the kingdom prepared for you from the foundation of the world" Matt 25:33-34.

Paul said, "24 For we are saved by hope: but hope that is seen is not hope: for what a man seeth, why doth he yet hope for? 25 But if we hope for that we see not, then do we with patience wait for it. 26 Likewise the Spirit also helpeth our infirmities: for we know not what we should pray for as we ought: but the Spirit itself maketh intercession for us with groanings which cannot be uttered. 27 And he that searcheth the hearts knoweth what is the mind of the Spirit, because he maketh intercession for the saints according to the will of God. 28 And we know that all things work together for good to them that love God, to them who are the called according to his purpose" Romans 8:24-28.

John, Peter, And Paul Explained To The Churches Of Christ; Concerning Faith, Hope, And Charity, And They Express That The Greatest Of Them Is Charity; Which Is A Gift Or A Contribution That People Give To Help Others.

Peter said, "44 And all that believed were together, and had all things common; 45 And sold their possessions and goods, and parted them to all men, as every man had need. 46 And they, continuing daily with one accord in the temple, and breaking bread from house to house, did eat their meat with gladness and singleness of heart, 47 Praising God, and having favour with all the people. And the Lord added to the church daily such as should be saved" Acts 2:44-47.

Paul said, "13 And now abideth faith, hope, charity, these three; but the greatest of these *is* charity" 1 Cor 13:13.

John said, "18 My little children, let us not love in word, neither in tongue; but in deed and in truth" 1 John 3:18.

John said, "16 For God so loved the world, that he gave his only begotten Son, that whosoever believeth in him should not perish, but have everlasting life John" 3:16.

The God Of Heaven That Cannot Lie, Promise Those That Hold On To The Hope Of Seeing Christ When He Come Again Unto The End, Will Receive Eternal Life.

Paul said, "1 Paul, a servant of God, and an apostle of Jesus Christ, according to the faith of God's elect, and the acknowledging of the truth which is after godliness; 2 In hope of eternal life, which God, that cannot lie, promised before the world began; 3 But hath in due times manifested his word through preaching, which is committed unto me according to the commandment of God our Saviour; 4 To Titus, mine own son after the common faith: Grace, mercy, and peace, from God the Father and the Lord Jesus Christ our Saviour" Titus 1:1-4.

The Hebrew writer said, "9 But, beloved, we are persuaded better things of you, and things that accompany salvation, though we thus speak. 10 For God is not unrighteous to forget your work and labour of love, which ye have shewed toward his name, in that ye have ministered to the saints, and do minister. 11 And we desire that every one of you do shew the same diligence to the full assurance of hope unto the end: 12 That ye be not slothful, but followers of them who through faith and patience inherit the promises" Heb 6:9-12.

Paul said, "1 Having therefore these promises, dearly beloved, let us cleanse ourselves from all filthiness of the flesh and spirit, perfecting holiness in the fear of God. 2 Receive us; we have wronged no man, we have corrupted no man, we have defrauded no man" 2 Cor 7:1-2.

Peter said, "1 Simon Peter, a servant and an apostle of Jesus Christ, to them that have obtained like precious faith with us through the righteousness of God and our Saviour Jesus Christ: 2 Grace and peace be multiplied unto you through the knowledge of God, and of Jesus our Lord, 3 According as his divine power hath given unto us all things that pertain unto life and godliness, through the knowledge of him that hath called us to glory and virtue: 4 Whereby are given unto us exceeding great and precious promises: that by these ye might be partakers of the divine nature, having escaped the corruption that is in the world through lust" 2 Peter 1:1-4.

Peter said, "13 Wherefore gird up the loins of your mind, be sober, and hope to the end for the grace that is to be brought unto you at the revelation of Jesus Christ; 14 As obedient children, not fashioning yourselves according to the former lusts in your ignorance: 15 But as he which hath called you is holy, so be ye holy in all manner of conversation; 16 Because it is written, Be ye holy; for I am holy" 1 Peter 1:13-16.

A Messenger From God

A Massinger Is A Person Who Transmit Information That Is Sent From One Person To Another.

God Sent A Messenger To Prepare The Way Before Him.

The Bible said, "1 Behold, I will send my messenger, and he shall prepare the way before me: and the Lord, whom ye seek, shall suddenly come to his temple, even the messenger of the covenant, whom ye delight in: behold, he shall come, saith the LORD of hosts. 2 But who may abide the day of his coming? and who shall stand when he appeareth? for he is like a refiner's fire, and like fullers' soap: 3 And he shall sit as a refiner and purifier of silver: and he shall purify the sons of Levi, and purge them as gold and silver, that they may offer unto the LORD an offering in righteousness. 4 Then shall the offering of Judah and Jerusalem be pleasant unto the LORD, as in the days of old, and as in former years" Mal 3:1-4.

The Bible said, "6 There was a man sent from God, whose name was John. 7 The same came for a witness, to bear witness of the Light, that all men through him might believe. 8 He was not that Light, but was sent to bear witness of that Light. 9 That was the true Light, which lighteth every man that cometh into the world" John 1:6-9.

The Bible said, "19 And this is the record of John, when the Jews sent priests and Levites from Jerusalem to ask him, Who art thou? 20 And he confessed, and denied not; but confessed, I am not the Christ. 22

Then said they unto him, Who art thou? that we may give an answer to them that sent us. What sayest thou of thyself? 23 He said, I am the voice of one crying in the wilderness, Make straight the way of the Lord, as said the prophet Esaias" John 1:19-20, 22-23.

God Sent A Messenger To Warn The People, Concerning The Judgment.

The Bible said, "5 And I will come near to you to judgment; and I will be a swift witness against the sorcerers, and against the adulterers, and against false swearers, and against those that oppress the hireling in his wages, the widow, and the fatherless, and that turn aside the stranger from his right, and fear not me, saith the LORD of hosts" Mal 3:5.

John said, "7 He that overcometh shall inherit all things; and I will be his God, and he shall be my son. 8 But the fearful, and unbelieving, and the abominable, and murderers, and whoremongers, and sorcerers, and idolaters, and all liars, shall have their part in the lake which burneth with fire and brimstone: which is the second death" Rev 21:7-8.

Jude said, "6 And the angels which kept not their first estate, but left their own habitation, he hath reserved in everlasting chains under darkness unto the judgment of the great day. 15 To execute judgment upon all, and to convince all that are ungodly among them of all their ungodly deeds which they have ungodly committed, and of all their hard speeches which ungodly sinners have spoken against him. 16 These are murmurers, complainers, walking after their own lusts; and their mouth speaketh great swelling words, having men's persons in admiration because of advantage. 17 But, beloved, remember ye the words which were spoken before of the apostles of our Lord Jesus Christ; 18 How that they told you there should be mockers in the last time, who should walk after their own ungodly lusts" Jude 1:6, 15-18.

God Sent A Messenger To Inform The People That They Had Gone Away From His Ordinances.

The Bible said, "7 Even from the days of your fathers ye are gone away from mine ordinances, and have not kept them. Return unto me, and I will return unto you, saith the LORD of hosts. But ye said, Wherein shall we return?" Mal 3:7.

The Bible said, "13 Your words have been stout against me, saith the LORD. Yet ye say, What have we spoken so much against thee? 14 Ye have said, It is vain to serve God: and what profit is it that we have kept his ordinance, and that we have walked mournfully before the LORD of hosts? 15 And now we call the proud happy; yea, they that work wickedness are set up; yea, they that tempt God are even delivered" Mal 3:13-15.

Stephen said, "51 Ye stiffnecked and uncircumcised in heart and ears, ye do always resist the Holy Ghost: as your fathers did, so do ye. 52 Which of the prophets have not your fathers persecuted? and they have slain them which shewed before of the coming of the Just One; of whom ye have been now the betrayers and murderers: 53 Who have received the law by the disposition of angels, and have not kept it" Acts 7:51-53.

The Bible said, "4 Ye shall do my judgments, and keep mine ordinances, to walk therein: I am the LORD your God. 5 Ye shall therefore keep my statutes, and my judgments: which if a man do, he shall live in them: I am the LORD" Lev 18:4-5.

Paul said, "2 Now I praise you, brethren, that ye remember me in all things, and keep the ordinances, as I delivered them to you. 3 But I would have you know, that the head of every man is Christ; and the head of the woman is the man; and the head of Christ is God" 1 Cor 11:2-3.

Peter said, "11 If any man speak, let him speak as the oracles of God; if any man minister, let him do it as of the ability which God giveth: that God in all things may be glorified through Jesus Christ, to whom be praise and dominion for ever and ever. Amen" 1 Peter 4:11.

God Sent A Messenger To Warn The People, About The Danger Of Robbing Him; And The Punishment That They Shall Receive For Doing So.

Malachi said, "8 Will a man rob God? Yet ye have robbed me. But ye say, Wherein have we robbed thee? In tithes and offerings. 9 Ye are cursed with a curse: for ye have robbed me, even this whole nation. 10 Bring ye all the tithes into the storehouse, that there may be meat in mine house, and prove me now herewith, saith the LORD of hosts, if I will not open you the windows of heaven, and pour you out a blessing, that there shall not be room enough to receive it. 11 And I will rebuke the devourer for your sakes, and he shall not destroy the fruits of your ground; neither shall your vine cast her fruit before the time in the field, saith the LORD of hosts. 12 And all nations shall call you blessed: for ye shall be a delightsome land, saith the LORD of hosts" Mal 3:8-12.

The Bible said, "1 But a certain man named Ananias, with Sapphira his wife, sold a possession, 2 And kept back part of the price, his wife also being privy to it, and brought a certain part, and laid it at the apostles' feet. 3 But Peter said, Ananias, why hath Satan filled thine heart to lie to the Holy Ghost, and to keep back part of the price of the land? 4 Whiles it remained, was it not thine own? and after it was sold, was it not in thine own power? why hast thou conceived this thing in thine heart? thou hast not lied unto men, but unto God. 5 And Ananias hearing these words fell down, and gave up the ghost: and great fear came on all them that heard these things" Acts 5:1-5.

The Bible said, "6 And the young men arose, wound him up, and carried him out, and buried him. 7 And it was about the space of three hours after, when his wife, not knowing what was done, came in. 8 And Peter answered unto her, Tell me whether ye sold the land for so much? And she said, Yea, for so much. 9 Then Peter said unto her, How is it that ye have agreed together to tempt the Spirit of the Lord? behold, the feet of them which have buried thy husband are at the door, and shall carry thee out. 10 Then fell she down straightway at his feet, and yielded up the ghost: and the young men came in, and found her dead, and, carrying her forth, buried her by her husband. 11 And great fear came upon all the church, and upon as many as heard these things" Acts 5:5-11.

God Sent A Messenger To Comfort Those Who Names Was Written In A Book Of Remembrance.

The Bible said, "16 Then they that feared the LORD spake often one to another: and the LORD hearkened, and heard it, and a book of remembrance was written before him for them that feared the LORD, and that thought upon his name. 17 And they shall be mine, saith the LORD of hosts, in that day when I make up my jewels; and I will spare them, as a man spareth his own son that serveth him. 18 Then shall ye return, and discern between the righteous and the wicked, between him that serveth God and him that serveth him not" Mal 3:16-18.

John said, "12 And I saw the dead, small and great, stand before God; and the books were opened: and another book was opened, which is the book of life: and the dead were judged out of those things which were written in the books, according to their works. 13 And the sea gave up the dead which were in it; and death and hell delivered up the dead which were in them: and they were judged every man according to their works. 14 And death and hell were cast into the lake of fire. This is the second death. 15 And whosoever was not found written in the book of life was cast into the lake of fire" Rev 20:12-15.

John said, "10 And he saith unto me, Seal not the sayings of the prophecy of this book: for the time is at hand. 11 He that is unjust, let him be unjust still: and he which is filthy, let him be filthy still: and he that is righteous, let him be righteous still: and he that is holy, let him be holy still. 12 And, behold, I come quickly; and my reward is with me, to give every man according as his work shall be. 18 For I testify unto every man that heareth the words of the prophecy of this book, If any man shall add unto these things, God shall add unto him the plagues that are written in this book: 19 And if any man shall take away from the words of the book of this prophecy, God shall take away his part out of the book of life, and out of the holy city, and from the things which are written in this book" Rev 22:10-12, 18-19.

What Kind Of Foundation Is Your Spiritual House Built Upon

The Bible Teaches That There Are Two Types Of Foundations That Man Build Upon.

The Wise Man Build His House Upon A Rock Foundation, Making It Strong, Safe, And Able To Stand Against The Storms Of Life, That Will Beat Upon That House.

Christ said, "24 Therefore whosoever heareth these sayings of mine, and doeth them, I will liken him unto a wise man, which built his house upon a rock: 25 And the rain descended, and the floods came, and the winds blew, and beat upon that house; and it fell not: for it was founded upon a rock" Matt 7:24-25.

Paul Laid The Foundation For Every Man To Build Thereupon.

The Bible said, "16 Therefore thus saith the Lord GOD, Behold, I lay in Zion for a foundation a stone, a tried stone, a precious corner stone, a sure foundation: he that believeth shall not make haste" Isaiah 28:16.

Paul said, "10 According to the grace of God which is given unto me, as a wise masterbuilder, I have laid the foundation, and another buildeth thereon. But let every man take heed how he buildeth thereupon. 11 For other foundation can no man lay than that is laid, which is Jesus Christ. 12 Now if any man build upon this foundation gold, silver, precious stones, wood, hay, stubble; 13 Every man's work shall be made manifest: for the day shall declare it, because it shall be revealed by fire; and the fire shall try every man's work of what sort it is. 14 If any man's work abide which he hath built thereupon, he shall receive a reward. 15 If any man's work shall be burned, he shall suffer loss: but he himself shall be saved; yet so as by fire" 1 Cor 3:10-15.

Peter Made It Plain That The Foundation That Paul Laid Was For To Build Up A Spiritual House Upon It.

Peter said, "5 Ye also, as lively stones, are built up a spiritual house, an holy priesthood, to offer up spiritual sacrifices, acceptable to God by Jesus Christ. 6 Wherefore also it is contained in the scripture, Behold, I lay in Sion a chief corner stone, elect, precious: and he that believeth on him shall not be confounded. 7 Unto you therefore which believe he is precious: but unto them which be disobedient, the stone which the builders disallowed, the same is made the head of the corner, 8 And a stone of stumbling, and a rock of offence, even to them which stumble at the word, being disobedient: whereunto also they were appointed" 1 Peter 2:5-8.

Peter Address Christians, As A Chosen Generation, A Royal Priesthood, An Holy Nation, A Peculiar People.

Peter said, "9 But ye are a chosen generation, a royal priesthood, an holy nation, a peculiar people; that ye should shew forth the praises of him who hath called you out of darkness into his marvellous light: 10 Which in time past were not a people, but are now the people of God: which had not obtained mercy, but now have obtained mercy. 11 Dearly beloved, I beseech you as strangers and pilgrims, abstain from fleshly lusts, which war against the soul" 1 Peter 2:9-11.

Peter said, "12 Having your conversation honest among the Gentiles: that, whereas they speak against you as evildoers, they may by your good works, which they shall behold, glorify God in the day of visitation. 13 Submit yourselves to every ordinance of man for the Lord's sake: whether it be to the king, as supreme; 14 Or unto governors, as unto them that are sent by him for the punishment of evildoers, and for the praise of them that do well. 15 For so is the will of God, that with well doing ye may put to silence the ignorance of foolish men" 1 Peter 2:12-15.

Paul Assured Timothy, That The Foundation Of God Stand Sure.

Paul said, "19 Nevertheless the foundation of God standeth sure, having this seal, The Lord knoweth them that are his. And, Let every one that nameth the name of Christ depart from iniquity. 20 But in a great house there are not only vessels of gold and of silver, but also of wood and of earth; and some to honour, and some to dishonour. 21 If a man therefore purge himself from these, he shall be a vessel unto honour, sanctified, and meet for the master's use, and prepared unto every good work" 2 Tim 2:19-21.

Peter Encourage The Older Christians, To Desire The Sincere Milk Of The Word, That They May Continue To Grow In The Word, As Well As The New Christians Do.

Peter said, "2 As newborn babes, desire the sincere milk of the word, that ye may grow thereby: 3 If so be ye have tasted that the Lord is gracious. 4 To whom coming, as unto a living stone, disallowed indeed of men, but chosen of God, and precious, 5 Ye also, as lively stones, are built up a spiritual house, an holy priesthood, to offer up spiritual sacrifices, acceptable to God by Jesus Christ" 1 Peter 2:2-5.

Paul Explained To The Churches of Christ, That They Were All A Part Of The Same Spiritual Rock, As Their Ancestors Were.

Paul said, "4 And did all drink the same spiritual drink: for they drank of that spiritual Rock that followed them: and that Rock was Christ. 5 But with many of them God was not well pleased: for they were overthrown in the wilderness. 6 Now these things were our examples, to the intent we should not lust after evil things, as they also lusted. 7 Neither be ye idolaters, as were some of them; as it is written, The people sat down to eat and drink, and rose up to play. 8 Neither let us commit fornication, as some of them committed, and fell in one day three and twenty thousand" 1 Cor 10:4-8.

The Foolish Man Built His House Upon The Sand Foundation, And When The Storms Of Life Come And Beat Upon That House, It Will Fall.

Christ said, "26 And every one that heareth these sayings of mine, and doeth them not, shall be likened unto a foolish man, which built his house upon the sand: 27 And the rain descended, and the floods came, and the winds blew, and beat upon that house; and it fell: and great was the fall of it" Matt 7:26-27.

Peter said, "21 Because that, when they knew God, they glorified him not as God, neither were thankful; but became vain in their imaginations, and their foolish heart was darkened. 22 Professing themselves to be wise, they became fools" Romans 1:21-22.

David said, "4 Blessed is that man that maketh the LORD his trust, and respecteth not the proud, nor such as turn aside to lies" Psalms 40:4.

The Bible Teaches That A House Divided Against Itself Cannot Stand.

Christ said, "25 And Jesus knew their thoughts, and said unto them, Every kingdom divided against itself is brought to desolation; and every city or house divided against itself shall not stand: 26 And if Satan cast out Satan, he is divided against himself; how shall then his kingdom stand?" Matt 12:25-26.

Paul said, "10 Now I beseech you, brethren, by the name of our Lord Jesus Christ, that ye all speak the same thing, and that there be no divisions among you; but that ye be perfectly joined together in the same mind and in the same judgment. 11 For it hath been declared unto me of you, my brethren, by them which are of the house of Chloe, that there are contentions among you. 12 Now this I say, that every one of you saith, I am of Paul; and I of Apollos; and I of Cephas; and I of Christ.

13 Is Christ divided? was Paul crucified for you? or were ye baptized in the name of Paul?" 1 Cor 1:10-13.

Paul, And The Hebrew Writer, Was Trying To Encourage Christians To Hold On To Their Profession.

Paul said, "12 Fight the good fight of faith, lay hold on eternal life, whereunto thou art also called, and hast professed a good profession before many witnesses. 13 I give thee charge in the sight of God, who quickeneth all things, and before Christ Jesus, who before Pontius Pilate witnessed a good confession; 14 That thou keep this commandment without spot, unrebukeable, until the appearing of our Lord Jesus Christ: 15 Which in his times he shall shew, who is the blessed and only Potentate, the King of kings, and Lord of lords" 1 Tim 6:12-15.

The Hebrew writer said, "1 Wherefore, holy brethren, partakers of the heavenly calling, consider the Apostle and High Priest of our profession, Christ Jesus; 2 Who was faithful to him that appointed him, as also Moses was faithful in all his house. 3 For this man was counted worthy of more glory than Moses, inasmuch as he who hath builded the house hath more honour than the house. 4 For every house is builded by some man; but he that built all things is God. 5 And Moses verily was faithful in all his house, as a servant, for a testimony of those things which were to be spoken after; 6 But Christ as a son over his own house; whose house are we, if we hold fast the confidence and the rejoicing of the hope firm unto the end" Heb 3:1-6.

The God Of Heaven Is Not Willing That Any Should Perish But That All Should Come To Repentance!

Peter said, "9 The Lord is not slack concerning his promise, as some men count slackness; but is longsuffering to us-ward, not willing that any should perish, but that all should come to repentance" 2 Peter 3:9.

The God Of Heaven Is Not Willing That Any Foolish Person Should Perish, But That They Would All Come To Repentance, In Order To Be Saved!

David said, "1 The fool hath said in his heart, There is no God. They are corrupt, they have done abominable works, there is none that doeth good. 2 The LORD looked down from heaven upon the children of men, to see if there were any that did understand, and seek God. 3 They are all gone aside, they are all together become filthy: there is none that doeth good, no, not one"
Psalms 14:1-3.

Solomon said, "2 A fool hath no delight in understanding, but that his heart may discover itself. 3 When the wicked cometh, then cometh also contempt, and with ignominy reproach" Prov 18:2-3.

Solomon said, "26 He that trusteth in his own heart is a fool: but whoso walketh wisely, he shall be delivered" Prov 28:26.

Isaiah said, "15 Because ye have said, We have made a covenant with death, and with hell are we at agreement; when the overflowing scourge shall pass through, it shall not come unto us: for we have made lies our refuge, and under falsehood have we hid ourselves" Isaiah 28:15.

Paul said, "25 For I would not, brethren, that ye should be ignorant of this mystery, lest ye should be wise in your own conceits; that blindness in part is happened to Israel, until the fulness of the Gentiles be come in. 26 And so all Israel shall be saved: as it is written, There shall come out of Sion the Deliverer, and shall turn away ungodliness from Jacob" Romans 11:25-26.

Paul said, "11 Now all these things happened unto them for ensamples: and they are written for our admonition, upon whom the ends of the world are come. 12 Wherefore let him that thinketh he standeth take heed lest he fall" 1 Cor 10:11-12.

Even Though Christ Came To Save Sinners, And Yet There Are Many Foolish People Who Will Not Consider, Nor Obey His Or God Plea.

Christ said, "28 Come unto me, all ye that labour and are heavy laden, and I will give you rest. 29 Take my yoke upon you, and learn of me; for I am meek and lowly in heart: and ye shall find rest unto your souls. 30 For my yoke is easy, and my burden is light" Matt 11:28-30.

Luke said, "10 For the Son of man is come to seek and to save that which was lost" Luke 19:10.

Luke said, "16 And he spake a parable unto them, saying, The ground of a certain rich man brought forth plentifully: 17 And he thought within himself, saying, What shall I do, because I have no room where to bestow my fruits? 18 And he said, This will I do: I will pull down my barns, and build greater; and there will I bestow all my fruits and my goods. 19 And I will say to my soul, Soul, thou hast much goods laid up for many years; take thine ease, eat, drink, and be merry. 20 But God said unto him, Thou fool, this night thy soul shall be required of thee: then whose shall those things be, which thou hast provided? 21 So is he that layeth up treasure for himself, and is not rich toward God" Luke 12:16-21.

The Bible said, "18 Come now, and let us reason together, saith the LORD: though your sins be as scarlet, they shall be as white as snow; though they be red like crimson, they shall be as wool. 19 If ye be willing and obedient, ye shall eat the good of the land: 20 But if ye refuse and rebel, ye shall be devoured with the sword: for the mouth of the LORD hath spoken it" Isaiah 1:18-20.

The Truth

Spiritually Speaking; Truth Is The Infallible Proof Of The Word Of God

The Truth; Can And Will Make People Holy, Completely Free From Sin

Christ said, "17 Sanctify them through thy truth: thy word is truth. 18 As thou hast sent me into the world, even so have I also sent them into the world. 19 And for their sakes I sanctify myself, that they also might be sanctified through the truth" John 17:17-19.

The Bible said, "31 Then said Jesus to those Jews which believed on him, If ye continue in my word, then are ye my disciples indeed; 32 And ye shall know the truth, and the truth shall make you free. 36 If the Son therefore shall make you free, ye shall be free indeed" John 8:31-32, 36.

The Truth; Will Accomplish Whatsoever The Word Of God Say.

Isaiah said, "10 For as the rain cometh down, and the snow from heaven, and returneth not thither, but watereth the earth, and maketh it bring forth and bud, that it may give seed to the sower, and bread to the eater: 11 So shall my word be that goeth forth out of my mouth: it shall not return unto me void, but it shall accomplish that which I please, and it shall prosper in the thing whereto I sent it. 12 For ye shall go out with joy, and be led forth with peace: the mountains and the hills shall break forth before you into singing, and all the trees of the field shall clap their hands. 13 Instead of the thorn shall come up the fir tree, and instead of the brier shall come up the myrtle tree: and it shall be to the LORD for a name, for an everlasting sign that shall not be cut off" Isaiah 55:10-13.

The Truth; Is Full Of Grace And Mercy.

John said, "14 And the Word was made flesh, and dwelt among us, (and we beheld his glory, the glory as of the only begotten of the Father,) full of grace and truth. 15 John bare witness of him, and cried, saying, This was he of whom I spake, He that cometh after me is preferred before me: for he was before me. 16 And of his fulness have all we received, and grace for grace. 17 For the law was given by Moses, but grace and truth came by Jesus Christ" John 1:14-17.

David said, "41 Let thy mercies come also unto me, O LORD, even thy salvation, according to thy word. 42 So shall I have wherewith to answer him that reproacheth me: for I trust in thy word. 43 And take not the word of truth utterly out of my mouth; for I have hoped in thy judgments. 44 So shall I keep thy law continually for ever and ever. 45 And I will walk at liberty: for I seek thy precepts. 46 I will speak of thy testimonies also before kings, and will not be ashamed. 47 And I will delight myself in thy commandments, which I have loved. 48 My hands also will I lift up unto thy commandments, which I have loved; and I will meditate in thy statutes" Psalms 119:41-48.

The Truth; Of The Word Of God Can, And Will, Strengthen The Souls Of All Mankind.

David said, "2 I will worship toward thy holy temple, and praise thy name for thy lovingkindness and for thy truth: for thou hast magnified thy word above all thy name. 3 In the day when I cried thou answeredst me, and strengthenedst me with strength in my soul. 4 All the kings of the earth shall praise thee, O LORD, when they hear the words of thy mouth" Psalms 138:2-4.

Paul said, "17 But God be thanked, that ye were the servants of sin, but ye have obeyed from the heart that form of doctrine which was delivered you. 18 Being then made free from sin, ye became the servants of righteousness. 19 I speak after the manner of men because of the infirmity of your flesh: for as ye have yielded your members servants to uncleanness and to iniquity unto iniquity; even so now yield your members servants to righteousness unto holiness. 20 For when ye were the servants of sin, ye were free from righteousness" Romans 6:17-20.

Even Though The Truth; Can And Will Make People Holy, Completely Free From Sin, There Are Still Some People, Who Rather Submit Themselves To The Lust Of The Devil.

Christ said, "44 Ye are of your father the devil, and the lusts of your father ye will do. He was a murderer from the beginning, and abode not in the truth, because there is no truth in him. When he speaketh a lie, he speaketh of his own: for he is a liar, and the father of it. 45 And because I tell you the truth, ye believe me not. 46 Which of you convinceth me of sin? And if I say the truth, why do ye not believe me? 47 He that is of God heareth God's words: ye therefore hear them not, because ye are not of God" John 8:44-47.

Isaiah said, "15 Because ye have said, We have made a covenant with death, and with hell are we at agreement; when the overflowing scourge shall pass through, it shall not come unto us: for we have made lies our refuge, and under falsehood have we hid ourselves: 16 Therefore thus saith the Lord GOD, Behold, I lay in Zion for a foundation a stone, a tried stone, a precious corner stone, a sure foundation: he that believeth shall not make haste" Isaiah 28:15-16.

Peter said, "14 Having eyes full of adultery, and that cannot cease from sin; beguiling unstable souls: an heart they have exercised with covetous practices; cursed children: 15 Which have forsaken the right way, and are gone astray, following the way of Balaam the son of Bosor, who loved the wages of unrighteousness; 16 But was rebuked for his iniquity: the dumb ass speaking with man's voice forbad the madness of the prophet. 17 These are wells without water, clouds that are carried with a tempest; to whom the mist of darkness is reserved for ever" 2 Peter 2:14-17.

The Truth; The Word Of God Teaches, That Those Who Hear And Believe The Preached Word Of God, And Resist The Devil, And Draw Close To God, He Will Save Them.

Paul said, "12 For there is no difference between the Jew and the Greek: for the same Lord over all is rich unto all that call upon him. 13 For whosoever shall call upon the name of the Lord shall be saved. 14 How then shall they call on him in whom they have not believed? and how shall they believe in him of whom they have not heard? and how shall they hear without a preacher?" Romans 10:12-14.

Christ said, "16 He that heareth you heareth me; and he that despiseth you despiseth me; and he that despiseth me despiseth him that sent me" Luke 10:16.

James said, "7 Submit yourselves therefore to God. Resist the devil, and he will flee from you. 8 Draw nigh to God, and he will draw nigh to you. Cleanse your hands, ye sinners; and purify your hearts, ye double minded. 9 Be afflicted, and mourn, and weep: let your laughter be turned to mourning, and your joy to heaviness. 10 Humble yourselves in the sight of the Lord, and he shall lift you up" James 4:7-10.

Joshua said, "15 And if it seem evil unto you to serve the LORD, choose you this day whom ye will serve; whether the gods which your fathers served that were on the other side of the flood, or the gods of the Amorites, in whose land ye dwell: but as for me and my house, we will serve the LORD. 16 And the people answered and said, God forbid that we should forsake the LORD, to serve other gods; 17 For the LORD our God, he it is that brought us up and our fathers out of the land of Egypt, from the house of bondage, and which did those great signs in our sight, and preserved us in all the way wherein we went, and among all the people through whom we passed: 18 And the LORD drave out from before us all the people, even the Amorites which dwelt in the land: therefore will we also serve the LORD; for he is our God. 19 And

Joshua said unto the people, Ye cannot serve the LORD: for he is an holy God; he is a jealous God; he will not forgive your transgressions nor your sins. 20 If ye forsake the LORD, and serve strange gods, then he will turn and do you hurt, and consume you, after that he hath done you good" Josh 24:15-20.

The Truth; The Word Of God Teaches, That The More God Bless Some People To Increase, The More They Sin Against Him.

Hosea said, "7 As they were increased, so they sinned against me: therefore will I change their glory into shame. 8 They eat up the sin of my people, and they set their heart on their iniquity. 9 And there shall be, like people, like priest: and I will punish them for their ways, and reward them their doings" Hosea 4:7-9.

The Bible said, "16 And he spake a parable unto them, saying, The ground of a certain rich man brought forth plentifully: 17 And he thought within himself, saying, What shall I do, because I have no room where to bestow my fruits? 18 And he said, This will I do: I will pull down my barns, and build greater; and there will I bestow all my fruits and my goods. 19 And I will say to my soul, Soul, thou hast much goods laid up for many years; take thine ease, eat, drink, and be merry. 20 But God said unto him, Thou fool, this night thy soul shall be required of thee: then whose shall those things be, which thou hast provided? 21 So is he that layeth up treasure for himself, and is not rich toward God" Luke 12:16-21.

Truth Is Forever On The Scaffold, Wrong Is Forever On The Throne, In The Mist Of All The Mischievous Dark Spirits Of The Devil, Sways The Future, God Standing In The Light Keeping Watch Over His Own: The Bible Is Right, Truth Planted In The Hearts Of Mankind, Will Rise Again.

Paul said, "3 Know ye not, that so many of us as were baptized into Jesus Christ were baptized into his death? 4 Therefore we are buried with him by baptism into death: that like as Christ was raised up from the dead by the glory of the Father, even so we also should walk in newness of life.

5 For if we have been planted together in the likeness of his death, we shall be also in the likeness of his resurrection: 6 Knowing this, that our old man is crucified with him, that the body of sin might be destroyed, that henceforth we should not serve sin" Romans 6:3-6.

Paul said, "16 For the Lord himself shall descend from heaven with a shout, with the voice of the archangel, and with the trump of God: and the dead in Christ shall rise first: 17 Then we which are alive and remain shall be caught up together with them in the clouds, to meet the Lord in the air: and so shall we ever be with the Lord. 18 Wherefore comfort one another with these words" 1 Thess 4:16-18.

A Part Of Paul's Spiritual Journey

Before Saul Was Call Paul, He Was Called Saul Of Tarsus.

The Bible said, "1 And Saul, yet breathing out threatenings and slaughter against the disciples of the Lord, went unto the high priest, 4 And he fell to the earth, and heard a voice saying unto him, Saul, Saul, why persecutest thou me? 8 And Saul arose from the earth; and when his eyes were opened, he saw no man: but they led him by the hand, and brought him into Damascus. 11 And the Lord said unto him, Arise, and go into the street which is called Straight, and enquire in the house of Judas for one called Saul, of Tarsus: for, behold, he prayeth" Acts 9:1, 4, 8, 11.

When Christ Intercepted Saul On His Journey To Damascus, Christ Change Saul Life Forever!

The Bible said, "6 And he trembling and astonished said, Lord, what wilt thou have me to do? And the Lord said unto him, Arise, and go into the city, and it shall be told thee what thou must do. 7 And the men which journeyed with him stood speechless, hearing a voice, but seeing no man. 8 And Saul arose from the earth; and when his eyes were opened, he saw no man: but they led him by the hand, and brought him into Damascus. 9 And he was three days without sight, and neither did eat nor drink" Acts 9:6-9.

The Bible said, "10 And there was a certain disciple at Damascus, named Ananias; and to him said the Lord in a vision, Ananias. And he said, Behold, I am here, Lord. 11 And the Lord said unto him, Arise, and go into the street which is called Straight, and enquire in the house of Judas for one called Saul, of Tarsus: for, behold, he prayeth, 12 And hath seen in a vision a man named Ananias coming in, and putting his hand on him, that he might receive his sight. 13 Then Ananias answered, Lord, I have heard by many of this man, how much evil he hath done to thy saints at Jerusalem: 14 And here he hath authority from the chief priests to bind all that call on thy name" Acts 9:10-14.

Saul Was A Chosen Vessel Unto The Lord, Before He Was Call Paul.

The Bible said, "15 But the Lord said unto him, Go thy way: for he is a chosen vessel unto me, to bear my name before the Gentiles, and kings, and the children of Israel: 16 For I will shew him how great things he must suffer for my name's sake. 17 And Ananias went his way, and entered into the house; and putting his hands on him said, Brother Saul, the Lord, even Jesus, that appeared unto thee in the way as thou camest, hath sent me, that thou mightest receive thy sight, and be filled with the Holy Ghost" Acts 9:15-17.

The Bible said, "18 And immediately there fell from his eyes as it had been scales: and he received sight forthwith, and arose, and was baptized. 19 And when he had received meat, he was strengthened. Then was Saul certain days with the disciples which were at Damascus. 20 And straightway he preached Christ in the synagogues, that he is the Son of God. 21 But all that heard him were amazed, and said; Is not this he that destroyed them which called on this name in Jerusalem, and came hither for that intent, that he might bring them bound unto the chief priests? 22 But Saul increased the more in strength, and confounded the Jews which dwelt at Damascus, proving that this is very Christ" Acts 9:18-22.

After Saul Was Baptized, He Was Call Paul.

The Bible said, "7 And upon the first day of the week, when the disciples came together to break bread, Paul preached unto them, ready to depart on the morrow; and continued his speech until midnight. 8

And there were many lights in the upper chamber, where they were gathered together. 9 And there sat in a window a certain young man named Eutychus, being fallen into a deep sleep: and as Paul was long preaching, he sunk down with sleep, and fell down from the third loft, and was taken up dead. 10 And Paul went down, and fell on him, and embracing him said, Trouble not yourselves; for his life is in him. 11 When he therefore was come up again, and had broken bread, and eaten, and talked a long while, even till break of day, so he departed. 12 And they brought the young man alive, and were not a little comforted" Acts 20:7-12.

Paul said, "28 And even as they did not like to retain God in their knowledge, God gave them over to a reprobate mind, to do those things which are not convenient; 29 Being filled with all unrighteousness, fornication, wickedness, covetousness, maliciousness; full of envy, murder, debate, deceit, malignity; whisperers, 30 Backbiters, haters of God, despiteful, proud, boasters, inventors of evil things, disobedient to parents, 31 Without understanding, covenantbreakers, without natural affection, implacable, unmerciful: 32 Who knowing the judgment of God, that they which commit such things are worthy of death, not only do the same, but have pleasure in them that do them" Romans 1:28-32.

Before Saul Was Call Paul, He Was A Notorious Persecutor Of Christ, And Of God, He Brought Christians, The People Of God, To Be Killed.

The Bible said, "58 And cast him out of the city, and stoned him: and the witnesses laid down their clothes at a young man's feet, whose name was Saul. 59 And they stoned Stephen, calling upon God, and saying, Lord Jesus, receive my spirit. 60 And he kneeled down, and cried with a loud voice, Lord, lay not this sin to their charge. And when he had said this, he fell asleep" Acts 7:58-60.

The Bible said, "1 And Saul, yet breathing out threatenings and slaughter against the disciples of the Lord, went unto the high priest, 2 And desired of him letters to Damascus to the synagogues, that if he found any of this way, whether they were men or women, he might bring them bound unto Jerusalem. 3 And as he journeyed, he came near Damascus: and suddenly there shined round about him a light from heaven: 4 And he fell to the earth, and heard a voice saying unto him, Saul, Saul, why persecutest thou me? 5 And he said, Who art thou, Lord? And the Lord said, I am Jesus whom thou persecutest: it is hard for thee to kick against the pricks" Acts 9:1-5.

After Saul Was Call Paul, He Went From Being A Notorious Persecutor Of Christ, And Of God; And From Bringing Christians To Be Killed: To Being A Reconciler Of God, And An Ambassadors For Christ, To Bring Sinners To God, To Be Saved.

2 Cor 5:18-21 18 And all things are of God, who hath reconciled us to himself by Jesus Christ, and hath given to us the ministry of reconciliation; 19 To wit, that God was in Christ, reconciling the world unto himself, not imputing their trespasses unto them; and hath committed unto us the word of reconciliation. 20 Now then we are ambassadors for Christ, as though God did beseech you by us: we pray you in Christ's stead, be ye reconciled to God. 21 For he hath made him to be sin for us, who knew no sin; that we might be made the righteousness of God in him.

Paul Explained The Condition That People Are In, When They Are Sold Under Sin.

Paul said, "14 For we know that the law is spiritual: but I am carnal, sold under sin. 15 For that which I do I allow not: for what I would, that do I not; but what I hate, that do I. 16 If then I do that which I would not, I consent unto the law that it is good. 17 Now then it is no more I that do it, but sin that dwelleth in me. 18 For I know that in me (that is, in my flesh,) dwelleth no good thing: for to will is present with me; but how to perform that which is good I find not" Romans 7:14-18.

Paul said, "19 For the good that I would I do not: but the evil which I would not, that I do. 20 Now if I do that I would not, it is no more I that do it, but sin that dwelleth in me. 21 I find then a law, that, when

I would do good, evil is present with me. 22 For I delight in the law of God after the inward man" Romans 7:19-22.

Paul said, "23 But I see another law in my members, warring against the law of my mind, and bringing me into captivity to the law of sin which is in my members. 24 O wretched man that I am! who shall deliver me from the body of this death? 25 I thank God through Jesus Christ our Lord. So then with the mind I myself serve the law of God; but with the flesh the law of sin" Romans 7:23-25.

Paul, The Hebrew Writer, And John, Tried To Encourage Christians, That We Would Not Allow Anyone, Or Anything, To Separate Us From The Love Of God: And Cause Him To Remove Our Candlestick.

Paul said, "35 Who shall separate us from the love of Christ? shall tribulation, or distress, or persecution, or famine, or nakedness, or peril, or sword? 36 As it is written, For thy sake we are killed all the day long; we are accounted as sheep for the slaughter. 37 Nay, in all these things we are more than conquerors through him that loved us. 38 For I am persuaded, that neither death, nor life, nor angels, nor principalities, nor powers, nor things present, nor things to come, 39 Nor height, nor depth, nor <u>any other creature</u>, shall be able to separate us from the love of God, which is in Christ Jesus our Lord" Romans 8:35-39.

Paul said, "8 We are troubled on every side, yet not distressed; we are perplexed, but not in despair; 9 Persecuted, but not forsaken; cast down, but not destroyed; 10 Always bearing about in the body the dying of the Lord Jesus, that the life also of Jesus might be made manifest in our body. 11 For we which live are alway delivered unto death for Jesus' sake, that the life also of Jesus might be made manifest in our mortal flesh. 12 So then death worketh in us, but life in you. 13 We having the same spirit of faith, according as it is written, I believed, and therefore have I spoken; we also believe, and therefore speak" 2 Cor 4:8-13.

Paul said, "14 Knowing that he which raised up the Lord Jesus shall raise up us also by Jesus, and shall present us with you. 15 For all things are for your sakes, that the abundant grace might through the thanksgiving of many redound to the glory of God. 16 For which cause we faint not; but though our outward man perish, yet the inward man is <u>renewed day by day</u>. 17 For our light affliction, which is but for a moment, worketh for us a far more exceeding and eternal weight of glory; 18 While we look not at the things which are seen, but at the things which are not seen: for the things which are seen are temporal; but the things which are not seen are eternal" 2 Cor 4:14-18.

The Hebrew writer said, "24 And let us consider one another to provoke unto love and to good works" Heb 10:24.

John said, "1 Unto the angel of the church of Ephesus write; These things saith he that holdeth the seven stars in his right hand, who walketh in the midst of the seven golden candlesticks; 2 I know thy works, and thy labour, and thy patience, and how thou canst not bear them which <u>are evil</u>: and thou hast tried them which say they are apostles, and are not, and hast found them liars: 3 And hast borne, and hast patience, and for my name's sake hast laboured, and hast not fainted. 4 Nevertheless I have somewhat against thee, because thou hast left thy first love. 5 Remember therefore from whence thou art fallen, and repent, and do the first works; or else I will come unto thee quickly, and will remove thy candlestick out of his place, except thou repent" Rev 2:1-5.

Paul, The Hebrew Writer, And James, Tried To Encourage Christians, To Run This Christian Race Without Wavering (Dodging In And Out).

Paul said, "24 Know ye not that they which run in a race run all, but one receiveth the prize? So run, that ye may obtain. 25 And every man that striveth for the mastery is temperate (self-controlled) in all things. Now they do it to obtain a corruptible crown; but we an incorruptible. 26 I therefore so run, not as uncertainly; so fight I, not as one that beateth the air: 27 But I keep under my body, and bring it into subjection: lest that by any means, when I have preached to others, I myself should be a castaway"1 Cor 9:24-27.

Paul said, "14 I press toward the mark for the prize of the high calling of God in Christ Jesus. 15 Let us therefore, as many as be perfect, be thus minded: and if in any thing ye be otherwise minded, God shall reveal even this unto you. 16 Nevertheless, whereto we have already attained, let us walk by the same rule, let us mind the same thing. 17 Brethren, be followers together of me, and mark them which walk so as ye have us for an ensample" Phil 3:14-17.

The Hebrew writer said, "23 Let us hold fast the profession of our faith without wavering; (for he is faithful that promised;)" Heb 10:23.

James said, "5 If any of you lack wisdom, let him ask of God, that giveth to all men liberally, and upbraideth not; and it shall be given him. 6 But let him ask in faith, nothing wavering. For he that wavereth is like a wave of the sea driven with the wind and tossed" James 1:5-6.

Paul Tried To Encourage Christians, To Learn And To Maintain The Knowledge Of The Word Of God.

Paul said, "6 For God, who commanded the light to shine out of darkness, hath shined in our hearts, to give the light of the knowledge of the glory of God in the face of Jesus Christ. 7 But we have this treasure in earthen vessels, that the excellency of the power may be of God, and not of us" 2 Cor 4:6-7.

Hosea said, "6 My people are destroyed for lack of knowledge: because thou hast rejected knowledge, I will also reject thee, that thou shalt be no priest to me: seeing thou hast forgotten the law of thy God, I will also forget thy children. 7 As they were increased, so they sinned against me: therefore will I change their glory into shame" Hosea 4:6-7.

Paul said, "7 Ever learning, and never able to come to the knowledge of the truth. 8 Now as Jannes and Jambres withstood Moses, so do these also resist the truth: men of corrupt minds, reprobate concerning the faith. 9 But they shall proceed no further: for their folly shall be manifest unto all men, as theirs also was" 2 Tim 3:7-9.

Paul Explained That He Wanted Recognition, Or Acknowledgment From The People, But He Had A Restriction, Or Constraint.

Paul said, "6 For though I would desire to glory, I shall not be a fool; for I will say the truth: but now I forbear, lest any man should think of me above that which he seeth me to be, or that he heareth of me. 7 And lest I should be exalted above measure through the abundance of the revelations, there was given to me a thorn in the flesh, the messenger of Satan to buffet me, lest I should be exalted above measure. 8 For this thing I besought the Lord thrice, that it might depart from me. 9 And he said unto me, My grace is sufficient for thee: for my strength is made perfect in weakness. Most gladly therefore will I rather glory in my infirmities, that the power of Christ may rest upon me. 10 Therefore I take pleasure in infirmities, in reproaches, in necessities, in persecutions, in distresses for Christ's sake: for when I am weak, then am I strong" 2 Cor 12:6-10.

Paul said, "13 Ye know how through infirmity of the flesh I preached the gospel unto you at the first. 14 And my temptation which was in my flesh ye despised not, nor rejected; but received me as an angel of God, even as Christ Jesus. 15 Where is then the blessedness ye spake of? for I bear you record, that, if it had been possible, ye would have plucked out your own eyes, and have given them to me. 16 Am I therefore become your enemy, because I tell you the truth?" Gal 4:13-16

Paul Sent Titus, And Another Brother, To The Christians In Corinth, Trying To Get Them To Repent.

Paul said, "18 I desired Titus, and with him I sent a brother. Did Titus make a gain of you? walked we not in the same spirit? walked we not in the same steps? 19 Again, think ye that we excuse ourselves unto you? we speak before God in Christ: but we do all things, dearly beloved, for your edifying. 20 For I fear, lest, when I come, I shall not find you such as I would, and that I shall be found unto you such as ye would not: lest there be debates, envyings, wraths, strifes, backbitings, whisperings, swellings, tumults: 21 And lest, when I come again, my God will humble me among you, and that I shall bewail many which have sinned already, and have not repented of the uncleanness and fornication and lasciviousness which they have committed" 2 Cor 12:18-21.

Paul, Peter, And John, Taught Christians, That With Love They Can Overcome All The Tricks Of The Devil, Which Can Cause Us To Lose Our Souls.

Paul said, "14 For all the law is fulfilled in one word, even in this; Thou shalt love thy neighbour as thyself. 15 But if ye bite and devour one another, take heed that ye be not consumed one of another. 16 This I say then, Walk in the Spirit, and ye shall not fulfil the lust of the flesh. 17 For the flesh lusteth against the Spirit, and the Spirit against the flesh: and these are contrary the one to the other: so that ye cannot do the things that ye would. 18 But if ye be led of the Spirit, ye are not under the law" Gal 5:14-18.

Peter said, "10 But chiefly them that walk after the flesh in the lust of uncleanness, and despise government. Presumptuous are they, selfwilled, they are not afraid to speak evil of dignities. 11 Whereas angels, which are greater in power and might, bring not railing accusation against them before the Lord. 12 But these, as natural brute beasts, made to be taken and destroyed, speak evil of the things that they understand not; and shall utterly perish in their own corruption; 13 And shall receive the reward of unrighteousness, as they that count it pleasure to riot in the day time. Spots they are and blemishes, sporting themselves with their own deceivings while they feast with you" 2 Peter 2:10-13.

John said, "17 Because thou sayest, I am rich, and increased with goods, and have need of nothing; and knowest not that thou art wretched, and miserable, and poor, and blind, and naked: 18 I counsel thee to buy of me gold tried in the fire, that thou mayest be rich; and white raiment, that thou mayest be clothed, and that the shame of thy nakedness do not appear; and anoint thine eyes with eyesalve, that thou mayest see.

19 As many as I love, I rebuke and chasten: be zealous therefore, and repent. 20 Behold, I stand at the door, and knock: if any man hear my voice, and open the door, I will come in to him, and will sup with him, and he with me. 21 To him that overcometh will I grant to sit with me in my throne, even as I also overcame, and am set down with my Father in his throne. 22 He that hath an ear, let him hear what the Spirit saith unto the churches" Rev 3:17-22.

Living A Guiltless Life

There Are Two Different Judging Systems For Mankind; One Is The Judicial System In The World; And One Is The Judicial System In The Church Of Christ.

In The Judicial System In The World, When A Person Commit A Crime, And The Jurors Deliberate Over The Crime That They Have Committed, And Come Up With A Guilty Verdict Against The Offender, Then The Judge Will Offer A Sentence For The Crime That They Have Committed; Even Though A Person Have Been Given A Guilty Verdict, Sometime Through A Retrial A Guilty Verdict Can Be Reversed, And Vindicated.

In The Judicial System In The Church Of Christ, When A Christian Commit A Sin, And It Have Been Proven By The People That That Person Is Guilty In The Sight Of God, That Person Must Pay The Penalty: Even Though A Christian Have Been Given A Guilty Verdict For Their Sin, If That Person Will Go To God In Repentance, And In Godly Sorrow, God Will Forgive, Reversed, And Vindicated That Person Sin.

The Bible said, "18 Come now, and let us reason together, saith the LORD: though your sins be as scarlet, they shall be as white as snow; though they be red like crimson, they shall be as wool. 19 If ye be willing and obedient, ye shall eat the good of the land: 20 But if ye refuse and rebel, ye shall be devoured with the sword: for the mouth of the LORD hath spoken it" Isaiah 1:18-20.

Paul said, "9 Now I rejoice, not that ye were made sorry, but that ye sorrowed to repentance: for ye were made sorry after a godly manner, that ye might receive damage by us in nothing. 10 For godly sorrow worketh repentance to salvation not to be repented of: but the sorrow of the world worketh death. 11 For behold this selfsame thing, that ye sorrowed after a godly sort, what carefulness it wrought in you, yea, what clearing of yourselves, yea, what indignation, yea, what fear, yea, what vehement desire, yea, what zeal, yea, what revenge! In all things ye have approved yourselves to be clear in this matter. 12 Wherefore, though I wrote unto you, I did it not for his cause that had done the wrong, nor for his cause that suffered wrong, but that our care for you in the sight of God might appear unto you" 2 Cor 7:9-12.

Spiritually Speaking; Living A Guiltless Sin Free Life, Means That You Are Living A Perfect Life In The Sight Of God.

The Bible said, "43 Ye have heard that it hath been said, Thou shalt love thy neighbour, and hate thine enemy. 44 But I say unto you, Love your enemies, bless them that curse you, do good to them that hate you, and pray for them which despitefully use you, and persecute you; 45 That ye may be the children of your Father which is in heaven: for he maketh his sun to rise on the evil and on the good, and sendeth rain on the just and on the unjust. 46 For if ye love them which love you, what reward have ye? do not even the publicans the same? 47 And if ye salute your brethren only, what do ye more than others? do not even the publicans so? 48 Be ye therefore perfect, even as your Father which is in heaven is perfect" Matt 5:43-48.

In Order For A Christians To Live A Guiltless Sin Free Life, They Must Forgive Those Who Have Sinned Against Them.

The Bible said, "9 After this manner therefore pray ye: Our Father which art in heaven, Hallowed be thy name. 10 Thy kingdom come. Thy will be done in earth, as it is in heaven. 11 Give us this day our daily bread. 12 And forgive us our debts, as we forgive our debtors. 13 And lead us not into temptation, but deliver us from evil: For thine is the kingdom, and the power, and the glory, for ever. Amen. 14 For if ye forgive men their trespasses, your heavenly Father will also forgive you: 15 But if ye forgive not men their trespasses, neither will your Father forgive your trespasses" Matt 6:9-15.

The Bible said, "3 Take heed to yourselves: If thy brother trespass against thee, rebuke him; and if he repent, forgive him. 4 And if he trespass against thee seven times in a day, and seven times in a day turn again to thee, saying, I repent; thou shalt forgive him. 5 And the apostles said unto the Lord, Increase our faith" Luke 17:3-5.

The Bible said, "1 Jesus went unto the mount of Olives. 2 And early in the morning he came again into the temple, and all the people came unto him; and he sat down, and taught them. 3 And the scribes and Pharisees brought unto him a woman taken in adultery; and when they had set her in the midst, 4 They say unto him, Master, this woman was taken in adultery, in the very act. 5 Now Moses in the law commanded us, that such should be stoned: but what sayest thou? 6 This they said, tempting him, that they might have to accuse him. But Jesus stooped down, and with his finger wrote on the ground, as though he heard them not. 7 So when they continued asking him, he lifted up himself, and said unto them, He that is without sin among you, let him first cast a stone at her" John 8:1-7.

The Bible said, "8 And again he stooped down, and wrote on the ground. 9 And they which heard it, being convicted by their own conscience, went out one by one, beginning at the eldest, even unto the last: and Jesus was left alone, and the woman standing in the midst. 10 When Jesus had lifted up himself, and saw none but the woman, he said unto her, Woman, where are those thine accusers? hath no man condemned thee? 11 She said, No man, Lord. And Jesus said unto her, Neither do I condemn thee: go, and sin no more" John 8:8-11.

In Order For A Person To Live A Guiltless Sin Free Life, They Have To Be Compassionate To Others.

The Bible said, "24 And when he had begun to reckon, one was brought unto him, which owed him ten thousand talents. 25 But forasmuch as he had not to pay, his lord commanded him to be sold, and his wife, and children, and all that he had, and payment to be made. 26 The servant therefore fell down, and worshipped him, saying, Lord, have patience with me, and I will pay thee all. 27 Then the lord of that servant was moved with compassion, and loosed him, and forgave him the debt" Matt 18:24-27.

It Is Detrimental, Or Dangerous To A Person Soul, If They Do Not Live A Guiltless Sin Free Life, And If They Are Not Compassionate To Others.

The Bible said, "28 But the same servant went out, and found one of his fellowservants, which owed him an hundred pence: and he laid hands on him, and took him by the throat, saying, Pay me that thou owest. 29 And his fellowservant fell down at his feet, and besought him, saying, 30 And he would not: but went and cast him into prison, till he should pay the debt" Matt 18:28-30.

The Bible said, "31 So when his fellowservants saw what was done, they were very sorry, and came and told unto their lord all that was done. 32 Then his lord, after that he had called him, said unto him, O thou wicked servant, I forgave thee all that debt, because thou desiredst me: 33 Shouldest not thou also have had compassion on thy fellowservant, even as I had pity on thee? 34 And his lord was wroth, and delivered him to the tormentors, till he should pay all that was due unto him. 35 So likewise shall my heavenly Father do also unto you, if ye from your hearts forgive not every one his brother their trespasses" Matt 18:31-35.

Jesus Christ Our Savior Lived, A Guiltless Sin Free Life, In The World.

The Bible said, "1 And the whole multitude of them arose, and led him unto Pilate. 2 And they began to accuse him, saying, We found this fellow perverting the nation, and forbidding to give tribute to Caesar, saying that he himself is Christ a King. 3 And Pilate asked him, saying, Art thou the King of the Jews? And he answered him and said, Thou sayest it. 4 Then said Pilate to the chief priests and to the people, I find no fault in this man" Luke 23:1-4.

Peter said, "20 For what glory is it, if, when ye be buffeted for your faults, ye shall take it patiently? but if, when ye do well, and suffer for it, ye take it patiently, this is acceptable with God. 21 For even hereunto were ye called: because Christ also suffered for us, leaving us an example, that ye should follow his steps: 22 Who did no sin, neither was guile found in his mouth: 23 Who, when he was reviled, reviled not again; when he suffered, he threatened not; but committed himself to him that judgeth righteously: 24 Who his own self bare our sins in his own body on the tree, that we, being dead to sins, should live unto righteousness: by whose stripes ye were healed. 25 For ye were as sheep going astray; but are now returned unto the Shepherd and Bishop of your souls" 1 Peter 2:20-25.

The Apostle Paul Lived, A Guiltless Sin Free Life, In The Church Of Christ.

Paul said, "7 I have fought a good fight, I have finished my course, I have kept the faith: 8 Henceforth there is laid up for me a crown of righteousness, which the Lord, the righteous judge, shall give me at that day: and not to me only, but unto all them also that love his appearing" 2 Tim 4:7-8.

Jesus Christ Is Coming Back After His Guiltless, Sin Free Church.

The Bible said, "21 Then said Jesus again unto them, I go my way, and ye shall seek me, and shall die in your sins: whither I go, ye cannot come. 24 I said therefore unto you, that ye shall die in your sins: for if ye believe not that I am he, ye shall die in your sins" John 8:21, 24.

Paul said, "25 Husbands, love your wives, even as Christ also loved the church, and gave himself for it; 26 That he might sanctify and cleanse it with the washing of water by the word, 27 That he might present it to himself a glorious church, not having spot, or wrinkle, or any such thing; but that it should be holy and without blemish" Eph 5:25-27.

Paul said, "17 But God be thanked, that ye were the servants of sin, but ye have obeyed from the heart that form of doctrine which was delivered you. 18 Being then made free from sin, ye became the servants of righteousness. 19 I speak after the manner of men because of the infirmity of your flesh: for as ye have yielded your members servants to uncleanness and to iniquity unto iniquity; even so now yield your members servants to righteousness unto holiness. 20 For when ye were the servants of sin, ye were free from righteousness. 21 What fruit had ye then in those things whereof ye are now ashamed? for the end of those things is death. 22 But now being made free from sin, and become servants to God, ye have your fruit unto holiness, and the end everlasting life. 23 For the wages of sin is death; but the gift of God is eternal life through Jesus Christ our Lord" Romans 6:17-23.

Moses Told The Army Of Israel, That If They Go Over Jordan And Let The Lord Fight For Them, Then They Will Return Guiltless Before The LORD.

The Bible said, "20 And Moses said unto them, If ye will do this thing, if ye will go armed before the LORD to war, 21 And will go all of you armed over Jordan before the LORD, until he hath driven out his enemies from before him, 22 And the land be subdued before the LORD: then afterward ye shall return, and be guiltless before the LORD, and before Israel; and this land shall be your possession before the LORD. 23 But if ye will not do so, behold, ye have sinned against the LORD: and be sure your sin will find you out" Num 32:20-23.

The People That Use The Name Of The Lord In Vain, And Those Who Worship The Lord In Vain, Shall Not Be Found Guiltless, And They Will Pay The Penalty For Doing So In The Day Of Judgment.

The Bible said, "7 Thou shalt not take the name of the LORD thy God in vain; for the LORD will not hold him guiltless that taketh his name in vain" Ex 20:7.

The Bible said, "7 Ye hypocrites, well did Esaias prophesy of you, saying, 8 This people draweth nigh unto me with their mouth, and honoureth me with their lips; but their heart is far from me. 9 But in vain they do worship me, teaching for doctrines the commandments of men" Matt 15:7-9.

The Seriousness Of Living And Dying In The Lord; And The Tragedy Of Living And Dying In Sin!

The World Needs To Know The Seriousness Of Living And Dying In The Lord; And The Tragedy Of Living And Dying In Sin!

Living In The Lord; Mean That You Have To Born Into Him By Baptism.

The Bible said, "3 Jesus answered and said unto him, Verily, verily, I say unto thee, Except a man be born again, he cannot see the kingdom of God. 4 Nicodemus saith unto him, How can a man be born when he is old? can he enter the second time into his mother's womb, and be born? 5 Jesus answered, Verily, verily, I say unto thee, Except a man be born of water and of the Spirit, he cannot enter into the kingdom of God" John 3:3-5.

Paul said, "1 What shall we say then? Shall we continue in sin, that grace may abound? 2 God forbid. How shall we, that are dead to sin, live any longer therein? 3 Know ye not, that so many of us as were baptized into Jesus Christ were baptized into his death? 4 Therefore we are buried with him by baptism into death: that like as Christ was raised up from the dead by the glory of the Father, even so we also should walk in newness of life" Romans 6:1-4.

Living In The Lord; Mean That You Have Put All Old Things Away.

Paul said, "17 Therefore if any man be in Christ, he is a new creature: old things are passed away; behold, all things are become new" 2 Cor 5:17.

Paul said, "4 Therefore we are buried with him by baptism into death: that like as Christ was raised up from the dead by the glory of the Father, even so we also should walk in newness of life. 5 For if we have been planted together in the likeness of his death, we shall be also in the likeness of his resurrection: 6 Knowing this, that our old man is crucified with him, that the body of sin might be destroyed, that henceforth we should not serve sin" Romans 6:4-6.

Living In The Lord; Mean That You Are Living A Perfect Sin Free Life.

The Bible said, "7 And the LORD said, I will destroy man whom I have created from the face of the earth; both man, and beast, and the creeping thing, and the fowls of the air; for it repenteth me that I have made them. 8 But Noah found grace in the eyes of the LORD. 9 These are the generations of Noah: Noah was a just man and perfect in his generations, and Noah walked with God" Gen 6:7-9.

The Bible said, "1 There was a man in the land of Uz, whose name *was* Job; and that man was perfect and upright, and one that feared God, and eschewed evil" Job 1:1.

Christ said, "48 Be ye therefore perfect, even as your Father which is in heaven is perfect" Matt 5:48.

Paul said, "27 To whom God would make known what is the riches of the glory of this mystery among the Gentiles; which is Christ in you, the hope of glory: 28 Whom we preach, warning every man, and teaching every man in all wisdom; that we may present every man perfect in Christ Jesus" Col 1:27-28.

Living In The Lord; Mean That You Are Living A Productive Life For Christ.

Christ said, "1 I am the true vine, and my Father is the husbandman. 2 Every branch in me that beareth not fruit he taketh away: and every branch that beareth fruit, he purgeth it, that it may bring forth more fruit. 3 Now ye are clean through the word which I have spoken unto you. 4 Abide in me, and I in you. As the branch cannot bear fruit of itself, except it abide in the vine; no more can ye, except ye abide in me. 5 I am the vine, ye are the branches: He that abideth in me, and I in him, the same bringeth forth much fruit: for without me ye can do nothing" John 15:1-5.

The Bible said, "23 But he that received seed into the good ground is he that heareth the word, and understandeth *it*; which also beareth fruit, and bringeth forth, some an hundredfold, some sixty, some thirty" Matt 13:23.

The Lord Is Pleading For People To Come Unto Him To Get Rest For Their Souls.

Christ said, "28 Come unto **me**, all ye that labour and are heavy **laden**, and **I** will give you **rest**. 29 Take my **yoke upon you**, and **learn of me**; for **I** am meek and lowly in **heart**: and **ye** shall **find rest unto your souls**. 30 For **my yoke is easy**, and **my burden is light**" Matt 11:28-30.

The Bible said, "16 For **God** so loved the **world**, that he gave his **only begotten Son**, that whosoever believeth in **him** should not **perish**, but have **everlasting life**. 17 For **God** sent not his **Son** into the world to **condemn the world**; but that the **world through him might** be **saved**" John 3:16-19.

Christ said, "9 I am the door: by me if any man enter in, he shall be saved, and shall go in and out, and find pasture. 10 The thief cometh not, but for to steal, and to kill, and to destroy: I am come that they might have life, and that they might have it more abundantly. 11 I am the good shepherd: the good shepherd giveth his life for the sheep" John 10:9-11.

Every Living Thing Will Die.

The Bible said, "19 There was a certain rich man, which was clothed in purple and fine linen, and fared sumptuously every day: 20 And there was a certain beggar named Lazarus, which was laid at his gate, full of sores, 21 And desiring to be fed with the crumbs which fell from the rich man's table: moreover the dogs came and licked his sores" Luke 16:19-21.

The Rich Man Experienced The Tragedy Of Living And Dying In Sin.

The Bible said, "22 And it came to pass, that the beggar died, and was carried by the angels into Abraham's bosom: the rich man also died, and was buried; 23 And in hell he lift up his eyes, being in torments, and seeth Abraham afar off, and Lazarus in his bosom. 24 And he cried and said, Father Abraham, have mercy on me, and send Lazarus, that he may dip the tip of his finger in water, and cool my tongue; for I am tormented in this flame" Luke 16:22-24.

Abraham Explain To The Rich Man Concerning The Lavish Lifestyle That He Had In His Lifetime.

The Bible said, "25 But Abraham said, Son, remember that thou in thy lifetime receivedst thy good things, and likewise Lazarus evil things: but now he is comforted, and thou art tormented. 26 And beside all this, between us and you there is a great gulf fixed: so that they which would pass from hence to you cannot; neither can they pass to us, that would come from thence" Luke 16:25-26.

The Rich Man Seeing How Severe The Tragedy Of Living And Dying In Sin, He Begged Abraham To Send Lazarus To Warn His Brothers Not To Come To Hell Where He Was.

The Bible said, "27 Then he said, I pray thee therefore, father, that thou wouldest send him to my father's house: 28 For I have five brethren; that he may testify unto them, lest they also come into this place of torment" Luke 16:27-28.

Abraham Reassured The Rich Man That His Brothers Can Escape The Tragedy Of Hell, By Hearing And Obeying The Word Of God From A Gospel Preacher.

The Bible said, "29 Abraham saith unto him, They have Moses and the prophets; let them hear them. 30 And he said, Nay, father Abraham: but if one went unto them from the dead, they will repent. 31 And he said unto him, If they hear not Moses and the prophets, neither will they be persuaded, though one rose from the dead" Luke 16:29-31.

John Explained To The Entire World The Tragedy Of Living And Dying In Sin.

The Bible said, "20 And the beast was taken, and with him the false prophet that wrought miracles before him, with which he deceived them that had received the mark of the beast, and them that worshipped his image. These both were cast alive into a lake of fire burning with brimstone" Rev 19:20.

The Bible said, "10 And the devil that deceived them was cast into the lake of fire and brimstone, where the beast and the false prophet are, and shall be tormented day and night for ever and ever. 14 And death and hell were cast into the lake of fire. This is the second death. 15 And whosoever was not found written in the book of life was cast into the lake of fire" Rev 20:10, 14-15.

The Bible said, "8 But the fearful, and unbelieving, and the abominable, and murderers, and whoremongers, and sorcerers, and idolaters, and all liars, shall have their part in the lake which burneth with fire and brimstone: which is the second death" Rev 21:8.

Prayer To God

My Prayer To God Is; To Give Him Thanks For Giving Me The Ability And The Opportunity To Write This Book, And I Thank Him For Giving My Wife The Ability To Help Me To Navigate Through Some Difficult Times.

My Prayer To God Is; To Give Him Thanks For Blessing You, The Readers Of This Book. And I Truly Hope That It Will Help You To Become Stronger In Your Spiritual Walk Of Life, And I Hope That It Will Inspire All Of You To Pass This Book On To Your Family And Friends.

My Prayer To God Is; That All Christians Will Pray And Ask God To Give Us Our Daily Bread, And To Forgive Us Our Debts, As We Forgive Our Debtors, And To Lead Us Not Into Temptation, But Deliver Us From Evil.

My Prayer To God Is; Not Only For Christians To Be Saved, But Also For Those Who Have A Zeal Of God, And Those Who Believe In Christ Through His Word, That We All May Be One In Christ Jesus Our Lord.

My Prayer To God Is; That Christians, Will Not Allow The Biases And The Prejudices Of Others, Or Ourselves To Cause Us To Lose Our Confidence, Or To Stop Us From Rejoicing In Love, And From Waiting On Christ Jesus Firm Unto The End.

My Prayer To God Is; That All Gospel Preachers Who Are Representing The Physician Of God, Will Continue To Administer The Balm Or The Medicine Of His Word Which Work Quicker, And Is More Powerful, And Sharper Than Any Surgical Equipment, Operating And Cutting Out The Sin That Is In The Soul, The Spirit, The Joints And Marrow, And In The Thoughts Of Our Hearts, Healing Us Immediately Through The Power Of His Word.

My Prayer To God Is; That His Grace And His Love, And The Love Of The Lord Jesus Christ, His Goodness, And His Mercy, And The Communion Of The Holy Ghost, Shall Rule And Abide Within Us, And That We Will Stay In The Church Of Christ Forever.

www.ingramcontent.com/pod-product-compliance
Lightning Source LLC
Chambersburg PA
CBHW030549080526
44585CB00012B/318